WORLD HERITAGE SITES IN CHINA

CHINA INTERCONTNENTAL PRESS

图书在版编目(CIP)数据

中国的世界遗产／《中国的世界遗产》编委会编．—北京：五洲传播出版社，2003.5
ISBN 7-5085-0226-4

Ⅰ．中...
Ⅱ．国...
Ⅲ．①名胜古迹—简介—中国—英文
②自然保护区—简介—中国—英文
Ⅳ．①K928.7 ②S759.992

中国版本图书馆CIP数据核字（2003）第038333号

顾　　问　赵启正
策　　划　李　冰
主　　编　郭长建
副 主 编　李向平　吴　伟
执行主编　宋坚之
图片主编　茹遂初
撰　　文　冯凌宇　陈　阳　隋　影　刘　耘
翻　　译　李竹润　刘　影　朱　明　杨　毅　朱　渊

责任编辑　冯凌宇
装　　帧　郑方红
版式设计　林　泉
图像处理　钟少欢

监　　制　国务院新闻办公室
出版发行　五洲传播出版社
地　　址　北京北三环中路31号
邮　　编　100088
电　　话　(86-10)82008396
制　　作　北京天人鉴设计制作有限公司
印　　刷　深圳雅昌彩色印刷有限公司
版　　次　2003年10月第1版第1次印刷
开　　本　230mm × 305mm　8开　31.5印张
字　　数　90千字
定　　价　296.00元

CONTENTS

序

联合国教科文组织北京办事处代表　青岛泰之

世界遗产是人类的宝贵记忆，具有物质和文化价值上不可代替、不可再现的性质。对于一个国家或民族来说，自然、文化遗产首先是历史的见证，同时也为其文明的延续、发展提供了无尽的原动力和精神资源；另一方面，世界遗产又是人类的共同财富，对促进不同国家、民族和文化类型之间人们的交流、理解及其共同繁荣有着重要的辅助作用。有组织、有计划地整理和保护全世界范围内的文化和自然遗产，是人类不容推卸的共同责任，也体现对历史、传统和一切文明成果的尊重。联合国教科文组织大会于1972年颁布《世界文化与自然遗产保护公约》，就是秉承了这样的宗旨。

中国是一个文明古老悠久、历史遗存丰厚、自然风光壮丽的国度，自1985年加入《世界文化与自然遗产保护公约》以来，已经成为发掘、研究和保护文化和自然遗产的一支积极力量。至2003年6月为止，中国共有28处文物古迹和自然景观列入“世界遗产名录”，一种艺术形式列入“人类口头和非物质遗产代表作”，目前还在积极进行遗产的申报工作。

中国的文化和自然遗产不仅属于中国，也属于全世界、全人类。我们面前的这本《中国的世界遗产》大型画册，就是对这28处遗产的全面、集中的展示。它不仅以精美的图片资料表现了中国的世界遗产的独特价值，还以生动的文字介绍了与之相关的文物、历史、地理、自然知识，帮助读者了解中国在数千年历史中形成的文化形态、政治理想、道德观念、哲学思想、美学追求、生活情趣，甚至中国的民族精神与民族性格，启发人们思考向传统文化和浩茫自然汲取滋养与力量的意义所在。相信它会赢得读者的喜爱。

联合国教科文组织对中国在保护人类文化和自然遗产方面所作的努力表示赞许。希望这本画册的出版更能对此有所助益。

青島泰之

Foreword

Yasuyuki Aoshima

Director and Representative UNESCO Office Beijing

World Heritage is a treasured memory for humanity. Their material and cultural value is irreplaceable and irretrievable. For a nation and a people, natural and cultural heritage primarily serves as testimony to a history. In addition, it is a driving force and a source of inspiration for the continued development of that civilization.

At the same time, World Heritage is a collective wealth shared by humanity that is instrumental in helping to facilitate exchange, understanding and a growing success shared between countries, peoples and cultures. Humanity must not ignore a mutual responsibility to sort and protect cultural and natural heritage throughout the world through organization and planning, and to show respect for the history, traditions and achievements of all civilizations. In 1972, the General Conference of UNESCO approved the "Convention Concerning the Protection of World Cultural and Natural Heritage" precisely to achieve this aim.

As a country with an ancient civilization, a rich historical legacy and magnificent natural scenery, China has already become an active force in the discovery, research and protection of cultural and natural heritage since ratifying the "Convention Concerning the Protection of World Cultural and Natural Heritage" in 1985. As of June, 2003, China had 28 cultural relic sites and natural landscapes on the "World Heritage List", one artistic contribution included in the "Masterpieces of the Oral and Intangible Heritage of Humanity", and is still pursuing the heritage application process.

China's cultural and natural heritage belongs not only to China but to the whole world and all of humanity. This book, "China's World Heritage", is a large-scale pictorial that focuses at length on these 28 legacies. Lively descriptions introducing the related cultural items, history, geography and natural expertise are accompanied by exquisite photographs displaying the unique value of China's World Heritage. They help the reader to understand the shape of Chinese culture developed over thousands of years, political ideology, moral concepts, philosophical ideas, aesthetic pursuits, life interests and even the conduct and spirit of the Chinese people. They also inspire people to think about the meaning of traditional culture and the natural environment as a source of power and sustenance in a way we trust will gain the reader's support.

UNESCO embraces China's efforts to safeguard the cultural and natural heritage of mankind. It is our hope that the publication of this pictorial will act as further encouragement.

Y. Aoshima

The Great Wall

As many see it, the Great Wall is the symbol of the Chinese nation.

The Great Wall was not built in a day. It is "great" in terms of both distance and time. From the 7th century BC to the 17th century AD, more than 10 dynasties were involved in building and rebuilding of the Great Wall. The different sections of the Great Wall built in different dynasties are different in length and location. Therefore, if one wants to know how long the Great Wall is, one must tell which dynasty's Great Wall one refers to.

The Great Wall as we see today is basically the wall rebuilt or renovated in the Ming Dynasty (1368-1644). Renovation of the old Great Wall started almost immediately after the dynasty was established and the project lasted until 1600, 44 years before it collapsed. The Great Wall of the Ming Dynasty starts at Mt. Hushan of eastern Liaoning Province in the east and ends at Jiayuguan Pass in Gansu Province in the west, snaking through Liaoning, Hebei, Tianjin, Beijing, Shanxi, Inner Mongolia, Shaanxi, Ningxia and Gansu provinces, with a total length of 6,700 kilometers. The project was also the last largest renovation of the Great Wall in history. The Great Wall of the Ming Dynasty is even 400 kilometers longer than China's longest river, the Yangtze.

Ruins of the Great Wall built or renovated in other dynasties can still be seen in central and north China. The earliest Great Wall was built in 656 BC - maybe even earlier -- in the State of Chu. Separate states tore apart the nation at the time as they fought wars with each other. The Great Wall of the Chu Kingdom was built for military defense and proved to be effective. Then other states started to build similar walls. The walls built by different states vary in length, ranging from a few hundred kilometers to one or two thousand.

All these walls failed to block the advance of armies of the Qin State. In the year 221 BC, Emperor Shihuang unified the country and established the Qin, China's first feudal dynasty. For a time, those walls seemed no longer necessary. However, the nomadic Xiongnu ethnic group in the north, or the "Huns" as referred to in the West, often made incursions into the Qin territory. To defend the empire's northern borders, Emperor Shihuang ordered a project to connect the defense walls in the north. That is how the Great Wall or the "Great Wall of ten Thousand *Li*" came into being, extending east to west for well over 5,000 kilometers.

The Qin Dynasty collapsed in 206 BC, and was succeeded by the Han, which was to rule China until 220 AD. Invasions by the Xiongnu horsemen became even more frequent and intense during the early period of the new dynasty, even though there was intermittent peace. "The moon of the Qin Dynasty still shines over the border passes of the Han, and soldiers are yet to return from battles fought ten thousand *Li* away." These lines from a Tang Dynasty poem say something about what happened in China during that period. As a result, the Great Wall was extended further west and, at the same time, an "Outer Great Wall" - walls beyond sections of the Great Wall of the Qin Dynasty -was built. That brought to 10,000 kilometers the total length of what is broadly referred to as the "Great Wall". The Great Wall was designed as a defense system. In practice, however, it provided protection to the newly developed Silk Road as well.

Most ancient Chinese emperors were ethnic Hans. During Northern and Southern Dynasties (420-589), however, eight ethnic minority regimes ruled north China in succession. These regimes also built walls for defense. Wall building continued into the Song Dynasty (960-1279), Liao Dynasty (916-1125) and Jin Dynasty (1115-1234). Walls built in the Jin Dynasty totaled 4,000 kilometers long.

Scores of long walls were built in the various dynasties, which are collectively called the "Great Wall". Some were consolidated, some renovated, and some just deserted. For example, some sections of the Great Wall of the Ming Dy-

001

nasty were shifted several hundred kilometers south from their counterparts of the Qin Dynasty. Experts estimate that the Great Walls built in the past 2,000 years, if put together, can be as long as 50,000 kilometers.

Building or renovation of the Great Wall was a time consuming project, and required a immeasurably huge input of human, financial and material resources. Some walls were repeatedly renovated. Was it possible that the various dynasties gave up building or renovating the walls? Did they have any defensive solutions more effective than the Great Wall? These questions have been debated until today.

We can find in the Chinese map that the Great Wall mostly coincides with the natural demarcation line between the agricultural area of China and its pastureland. Almost in every dynasty, the nomadic ethnic groups would invade the south. They were good at shooting arrows and had very good mobility on horsebacks. They would run away when chased, and would come back immediately after the defense forces withdrew. Even with the Great Wall at their disposal, central government troops would find it hard to defend the vast expanses of pastureland and desert in the north. Besides, logistics could hardly be guaranteed. Despite these and other difficulties, the Great Wall was extended and renovated again and again. It is believed that for invaders, surmounting the Great Wall would be costly in terms of time and logistics, and that even if they succeeded in doing that, the central government would have enough time to amass troops and fight back.

The Great Wall was quiet in the Tang (618-907), Yuan (1279-1368) and Qing (1644-1911) dynasties. In the year 628, when some court officials proposed that the Great Wall be renovated, Emperor Taizong of the Tang Dynasty said a downright no: "I don't need such a project to wipe away the enemies from the desert." The Yuan and Qing dynasties were established by nomadic ethnic groups from the north, and therefore they had the vast territory of pastureland and desert in the north under very good control. So they had never brought the renovation or rebuilding of the Great Wall on their agenda.

Natural topography was made good use of in the building of the Great Wall. No matter how hard the working conditions were, the Great Wall would be built wherever the topography is of strategic importance or with difficult access. In terms of engineering technology and defense facilities, the Great Wall of the Ming Dynasty was the best. Sections of the Great Wall around Beijing were the most important because it formed the fortification line in defense of the capital. Those sections of the Great Wall, which have become tourist spots today such as Badaling, Jinshanling, Mutianyu and Simatai sections, the Shanhaiguan Pass in Hebei Province and Huangyaguan Pass in Tianjin, all belonged to fortification line to the north of the capital.

Most sections of the Great Wall of the Ming Dynasty were built with bricks and stones, and some were built with rammed earth. The sections of the Great Wall in Beijing, Hebei, Shanxi and Gansu are seven to eight meters high on the average, and four to five meters wide on the top. On the top of the wall, the outside defense wall is about two meters high with battlements for shooting arrows and watching. In order to shoot those enemies down at the bottom of the wall, some projecting platforms with battlements were built every little distance. In addition, watchtowers were built on the wall. The towers usually have two stories. The upper floor is a platform for watching and fighting and the ground floor is for storing weapons and supplies and also for soldiers to stay.

Passes were built along sections of the Great Wall, at important crossings and where mountains and sea meet. There are as many as more than 1,000 passes along the Great Wall of the Ming Dynasty and the best known include

Shanhaiguan Pass that faces the Bohai Sea in what is now Hebei Province, Juyongguan Pass near Beijing and Jiayuguan Pass in Gansu Province, China's far west. In between those big passes, there are smaller passes. Some important passes had several fortification lines for each. For example, the Badaling section of the Great Wall was, in fact, the most important fortification line of Jurongguan Pass.

Beacon towers were built along the Great Wall every certain distance. Once enemy came, soldiers on the beacon towers would light signal fires at night and smoke in the daytime to send a message. In the Ming Dynasty, soldiers would fire cannons to signal alarm when the enemy came. When 100 enemy soldiers were spotted, soldiers at a beacon tower would fire one cannon shot and light a wisp of smoke. When some 500 enemy soldiers came, two cannon gun shots would be fired and two wisps of smoke lit. When more enemy soldiers came, more cannon shots would be fired and more wisps of smoke lit.

So the Great Wall is not just a wall but a military defensive system including passes, watchtowers, barracks and beacon towers. Different sections were defended by different military units in the Ming Dynasty, and the entire Great Wall was divided into nine military zones, which together had about one million soldiers under their command.

In order to solve the problem of military supplies, farmers were immigrated to the frontier areas to do farming while building the Great Wall. Besides, soldiers also took part in farming in their spare time. The barren and bleak frontier area therefore gradually turned into towns and cities. Fighting was temporary, and often times, the gate of a pass would be kept open. Battlefields would be turned into markets. People from outside the pass would bring in their horses, sheep or furs in exchange for grain, tea, cotton, silk and cloth. Such business was carried out either between folks or on official basis. Exchanges had also been conducted in such fields as production, culture and customs. As a result, connection between the nomadic ethnic groups and farming civilizations in the central plain was becoming more and more close.

The Great Wall was inscribed on the UNESCO list of World Cultural Heritage in 1987.

001 The Simatai section of the Great Wall in Beijing.

002 The Jiankou section of the Great Wall in Beijing. The Great Wall we see today is largely left over from the Ming Dynasty (1368-1644).

002

003

004

003 The Badaling section of the Great Wall in Beijing. As a part of the defense system for the capital, it is especially strong and complete and therefore representative of what is known as the Great Wall of the Ming Dynasty.

004 Watchtower atop the Simatai section of the Great Wall, Beijing. It is also known as the "Capital-Viewing Watchtower" because in ancient times, those on the tower had a clear view of Beijing in a fine day.

005 Ruins of a section of the Great Wall belonging to the Han Dynasty (206BC-220AD). Three "Great Walls" were built in different dynasties, the wall of the Han being 10,000 kilometers in length.

006 Ruins of a section of the Great Wall belonging to the Qin Dynasty (221BC-206BC). The Great Wall of the Qin is about 5,000 kilometers long.

005

006

008

009

007 The Jinshanling section of the Great Wall that dates back to the Ming Dynasty.

008 The Jiayuguan Pass is where the Ming Dynasty Great Wall ends in the west. Jiayuguan was an important hub of communication on the Silk Road that linked ancient China with countries and regions to its west.

009 Photo shows the Wohushan section of the Great Wall, on an ancient pathway that linked China's northeast and Mongolian grasslands to the north of the national capital.

010

011

012

010 A full view of the Jinshanling section of the Great Wall in mist.

011 Ruins of the Hengshan Castle on a section of the Great Wall in Ningxia Hui Autonomous Region, northwest China.

012 Photo shows a large bundle of straw left over from 2,000 years ago, which was to be used for lighting signal fire. It was found near a beacon tower on a section of the Great Wall near Dunhuang, Gansu Province, northwest China.

Imperial Palace of the Ming and Qing Dynasties

The Forbidden City in Beijing was the imperial palace of the Ming (1368-1644) and Qing (1644-1911) dynasties. Ancient Chinese believed that the Heavenly Emperor, the supreme ruler of the universe, lived in what they perceived as the "Purple Star", or the "Purple Palace", to which human beings were forbidden. Chinese emperors ruled the country in the name of Heaven, in their capacity as "Son of the Heaven". And, naturally, their living quarters were forbidden to commoners. That is why the palace complex in Beijing was called the "Forbidden City", or "Purple Forbidden City".

In 1406, Emperor Chengzu of the Ming Dynasty ordered construction of the Forbidden City and more than 100,000 workers and artisans were press-ganged to Beijing for the job. As the project progressed, a million workers were mobilized across the country to collect and transport the building materials. The grand project was completed in 1420. The following year, the imperial capital was moved from Nanjing to Beijing. While enjoying what their forefather had handed down to them, emperors of the succeeding generations ordered some expansion of the palace. Partial reconstruction was undertaken to repair damages done by fires.

The Forbidden City covers 720,000 square meters. Structures there that have been preserved to this day have a combined construction space of 150,000 square meters. More than 90 courtyards and 8,700 chambers are counted in the Forbidden City.

The grand palace complex is walled on four sides. The 10-meter high wall measures 960 meters from north to south and 752 meters from east to west. On each corner of the Forbidden City wall there stands a watchtower, majestic and beautiful. A 52-meter wide moat girdles the palace complex. The Forbidden City was built in such a way as to inspire awe and respect for China's supreme rulers.

Overlooking the Forbidden City from atop the Prospect Hill that faces its north gate across a street , one commands a clear view of the general layout of the Chinese capital. An 8.5-kilometer axis line runs through Beijing from south to north. The rectangular palace complex sits astride the axis line, at either side of which there stand, in symmetrical order, neat clusters of palace halls and courtyards. Glazed-tiled roofs of the imperial halls combine to present a majestic golden sea. The scene is especially glorious when the sun shines over the Forbidden City. Rows upon rows of one-story brick houses of the ordinary people outside the red wall serve to set off the grandeur and magnificence of the imperial dwelling. Today, any person can go to the Prospect Hill for a view of the Forbidden City. In feudal time, none could, because the Prospect Hill, now a park, was an imperial garden and was therefore forbidden.

In following the tradition, the Forbidden City is divided into two parts, the frontal part where the emperor worked on court affairs and the rear part, where the emperor and his family lived. The most important halls, those that served as venues of imperial audience and the most important ceremonies, are in the frontal part.

The Forbidden City has four gates. The main gate, the south-facing Meridian Gate, is in fact a tower on a wall with two wings, forming a square or courtyard in the shape of an inverted U in its front. There are five entrances in the frontal wall. The entrance in the center was reserved for the emperor exclusively. Court officials could use each of the other four entrances, according to their ranks. At the time, the ceremony to issue the calendar of the year was staged atop the Meridian Gate Rostrum. This was also where the emperor reviewed troops that had just returned victoriously from the battlefield, during which prisoners of war would be paraded in the square in front of his majesty. In the Ming Dynasty, court officials who happened to invoke anger of the emperor were often flogged on order of his majesty. The punishment

013

was carried out in the courtyard, below the Meridian Gate Rostrum.

In the frontal part of the Forbidden City, three grand halls – the Hall of Supreme Harmony, the Hall of Midway Harmony and the Hall of Perfect Harmony – stand on the axis line in neat order, from south to north. They represent the highest level of traditional Chinese wooden-structure architecture. Earthquakes happened time and again in the Ming and Qing dynasties, which destroyed many ordinary residential houses. The three halls, however, stood firm. Unfortunately, the three halls were burned down by fire ignited by lightning just one year after they were built. Experts say this is because the wooden structures are easy to catch fire and the halls stood high above the surrounding buildings without lightning rods. Fires broke out fairly frequently in the following centuries.

The Hall of Supreme Harmony sits on an eight-meter high terraced platform built with pure white marble. It faces a huge square more than 30,000 square meters in area. The hall has 72 wooden pillars. It is so large that it can be partitioned into 46 rooms, each covering 50 square meters. The height from the floor to the ceiling is 14.4 meters, as high as a three-story modern building.

The sizes, heights and shape of the roofs and furnishing of the palace buildings were strictly based on their respective ranks. The Hall of Supreme Harmony was of the highest rank. It was the venue for the most important ceremonies - those for enthroning new emperors and celebrating imperial birthdays and weddings as well as the most important festivals. An extremely elaborate, extravagant ceremony would be held when imperial audience was given. The emperor sat high in his throne, with court officials and the guard of honor standing in the square in front of the hall. Smoke from incense burning rose up in the air and the drums and gongs were beaten. All this helped create a divine and awesome atmosphere. Doubtless, this was exactly what the emperor wanted.

Before his majesty arrived in the Hall of Supreme Harmony, he usually stopped over in the Hall of Midway Harmony to get prepared or take a short rest. The day before a grand ceremony was held for worshiping of heaven or earth, the emperor would stay in the Hall of Midway Harmony to check and, if necessary, polish the draft elegiac address he was to deliver.

During the Ming Dynasty, the emperor habitually feted his court officials in the Hall of Perfect Harmony at the end of every lunar year. During the Qing Dynasty, however, the hall became the venue where imperial examinations were held to choose civil servants from among candidates who had worked their way up from examinations at the county and provincial levels.

In the rear part of the Forbidden City we find the Palace of Heavenly Purity, the Hall of Union and Peace and the Palace of Earthly Tranquility. Like the three great halls in the frontal part of the Forbidden City, these sit astride the axis line.

In the Ming Dynasty and early Qing Dynasty, the emperor and his queen lived in the Palace of Heavenly Purity. The fifth emperor of the Qing Dynasty, Emperor Yongzheng, however, moved to the Hall of Moral Cultivation, which also served as venue where he handled court affairs, received court officials and had audience with foreign envoys. Above the imperial throne in the hall hangs a horizontal board inscribed with the words "open and aboveboard." Starting from the Emperor Yongzheng, the practice that the emperor officially made public his heir in his lifetime was abolished. Instead, the emperor wrote the name of his heir in two copies. One was constantly with him and the other was hidden behind the tablet. The name of the new emperor would be announced after the old emperor died, by a leading court official.

The imperial living area has a garden fitted with an open-air theater. This must be the most pleasant part of the Forbidden City.

The three halls in the rear part of the Forbidden City sit on a terraced platform like the three great halls in the frontal part, and the two groups of halls look much the same in layout. But they are much smaller in size. Also, the distance between the buildings here is shorter. After all, the three halls in the frontal part of the Forbidden City were meant to inspire awe and respect for the imperial power. The three halls in the rear part were where their majesties ate, slept and entertained, and therefore they look more peaceful and less aggressive.

The Hall of Moral Cultivation does not sit astride the axis line. There are many stories about it. After the hall became the Emperor Yongzheng's living quarters, border wars broke out. On the emperor's order, a duty office was set up outside the southern wall of the hall, which was charged with assisting the emperor in handling emergencies. Three years afterwards, the office was renamed the "Council of State" which, comprising some of the most senior court ministers, was in fact the emperor's confidential secretariat. The council was directly responsible for the emperor. It was in fact the highest central government organ, lower in status only than the emperor.

Altogether, eight emperors, including Emperor Yongzheng, lived in the Hall of Moral Cultivation, where they also saw to state affairs. They had audience with court officials in the front wing of the hall. The east wing of the hall was where Empress Dowager Cixi attended court meetings from behind a screen, as an empress regent was supposed to be concealed from the sight of ministers. It was from here that she ruled the country for several decades of the late Qing Dynasty.

Altogether, 24 emperors of the two dynasties lived in the Forbidden City over a period spanning 500 years. You can tick them off on your fingers. But how much history can be retold and how much culture can be represented by the Forbidden City and its halls and gates? Nobody can tell.

The Forbidden City was listed as a site of World Cultural Heritage in 1987.

013 A bronze lion is placed at either side of a gate or a major hall in the Forbidden City, supposedly to guard the gate or hall while adding magnificence to it.

014 An aerial view of the Forbidden City. Structures in the Forbidden City are arranged in symmetrical order, the most important structures sitting astride the axis line of the complex and the less important, on either side of it. The third group of buildings seen from south to north in the picture forms the Meridian Gate, the main gate of the Forbidden City. To the north of the Meridian Gate we find the Hall of Supreme Harmony and other structures.

014

中华人民共和国万岁
世界人民大团结万岁

015

016

015 The Gate of Supreme Harmony is a nine-bay palace structure, its main gate in the middle with a gate at either side. The three gates form the entrance to the part of the Forbidden City occupied by the three main halls. A moat skirts the south part of the square in front of the Hall of Supreme Harmony.

016 The Imperial Road Stone in the north of the Hall of Perfect Harmony is 16 meters long, 3 meters wide and weighs more than 200 tons, the largest and heaviest carved stone in the Forbidden City. Nine dragons flying in the clouds are seen on it.

017 The Forbidden City is girdled by a 10-meter high wall. A watchtower is built atop each of the four corners of the wall. Outside the wall is the 52-meter wide moat round the Forbidden City.

017

018

019

018 The Hall of Supreme Harmony sits on a three-story, eight-mete-high, terraced platform of marble. This is the largest and most important building in the Forbidden City, the venue of imperial audience and the most important ceremonies during the Ming and Qing dynasties.

019 Photo shows the Hall of Midway Harmony and the Hall of Perfect Harmony. The former was where the emperor prepared himself for audience or ceremonies to be held in the Hall of Supreme Harmony. The latter was where the emperor feted court officials and gave interviews with successful candidates in imperial examinations.

020

021

022

020 The imperial throne in the Hall of Supreme Harmony. Pay attention to the nine dragons carved on it.

021 Gilded bronze vats are found in the Forbidden City, which were used to hold water as a precaution against fire.

022 The rear part of the Forbidden City, also known as the "Rear Court", served as the living quarters of the imperial family. It was also where the emperor handled the day-to-day court affairs. In this part of the forbidden City we find three main palace halls, which are blanked in the east and west by six halls where imperial concubines lived.

024

025

023 The Hall of Supreme Harmony measures 14 meters in height, from the floor to the ceiling. The roof is supported by 72 huge wooden pillars. The imperial throne is placed on a wooden terrace two meters high. The elaborate carvings add to the imperial majesty.

024 A glimpse of the Imperial Garden in the northernmost part of the Forbidden City.

025 The Palace of Preserved Elegance, one of the six side buildings in the rear part of the Forbidden City, which were imperial concubines' residences.

◀ 023

Mount Taishan

Mount Taishan is so famous [1] that it is regarded as the most sacred, most magnificent of the five sacred mountains in China, even though it is only the third highest. As many writers and poets acknowledge, Mount Taishan is beyond description, given its size and the numerous sites of historical and cultural interest on it. Meanwhile, they attribute its fame to both divine and human efforts. By "divine efforts", they refer to the strength of nature.

Rising majestically from a vast expanse of plain in central Shandong Province, the mountain stretches more than 200 kilometers from the east to the west and covers an area of 426 square kilometers. Looked from afar, the mountain, which has a broad base, sits there quietly, giving viewers an impression of steadiness and heaviness. No wonder we have the Chinese proverbs going like "as steadfast as Mount Taishan". In terms of elevation, its main peak, the Jade Emperor Peak, is just 1,545 meters above sea level. Located in the east of the North China plain, Mount Taishan is surrounded by hills with a plain of several hundred square kilometers immediately beyond. Ancient people had an inscriptions carved on a rock on the mountain, describing the mountain as "stretching as far as the horizon of the heaven, thrusting as high as the sky." Mount Taishan is so imposing, so awe inspiring, that far back to 2,500 years ago, an anonymous poet wrote of it, "Wherever they are, people in the state of Lu always have a full view of Mount Taishan."

Granite rocks are compared to bones and muscles of Mount Taishan, and pine trees, its soul, which combine to add sacredness to the mountain. Pine trees are old, many centuries old, but are strong and verdant. When wind sweeps through the forest, the pine trees would give a sough. When walking in the mountain trails in Autumn, one sees trails covered with golden pine needles while clouds are floating above. Tranquility permeates the entire mountain, occasionally broken by singing of birds and soughing of wind through the forest. Many pine trees have struggled themselves out of rock crevices and are strange looking. Together with the rocks and the mountain itself, pine trees present a unique landscape of its own.

Imposing as it is, Mount Taishan is beautiful with precipitous cliffs and deep gullies. On its top, people can have a full view of the sun rising from the Yellow River far beyond the horizon and sinking into it.

Beside its scenic beauty, Mount Taishan tops the list of the five sacred mountains for a wealth of cultural relics on it.

In the year 219 BC, Emperor Shihuang, the first emperor of the Qin, the first feudal dynasty to rule a unified China, climbed to the top of Mount Taishan. He had an altar built with earth to offer sacrifices to Heaven, at a ceremony he chose to call "feng". Then he descended the mountain, and had another altar built on a small hill to offer sacrifices to Earth, at a ceremony he called "shan". He did this to express his gratitude to Heaven and Earth and pray for consolidation of his dynasty. These imperial ceremonies, which made Mount Taishan special in status, were to be repeated in all dynasties after the Qin.

In the year 110 BC, Emperor Wudi of the Han Dynasty (206 BC -220 AD) climbed up Mount Taishan for the first time, and he came seven times in the following 22 years. Standing on top of the highest peak of Mount Taishan, so say historical records, the emperor claimed: "So high, the

026

highest; so large, the largest; so great, the greatest, about which I am so surprised!"

Under an established feudal rule, the thanks-giving ceremonies known as "feng" and "shan" could be held only when the country was unified and in peace, or after auspicious omens were observed. However, some good-for-nothing emperors defied the rule and went to the mountain for worshipping all the same. Emperor Zhenzong of the Song Dynasty (960-1279) was one of them. He ordered a "heavenly book" concocted in 1008, saying that Heaven had bestowed the imperial crown upon him and would protect the dynasty forever. He had the "heavenly book", so to speak, displayed at a ceremony for worshipping of the mountain. The true fact is that the country was chaotic under his reign. The ceremony was the last personally attended by an emperor in honor of Mount Taishan. Emperors of the later dynasties just sent their envoys to the mountain to offer sacrifices to the God of Mount Taishan. However, Heaven worshipping continued, at the Temple of Heaven in Beijing as in the case of Ming and Qing dynasties spanning more than 500 years until China became a republic in 1911. Some emperors took a special liking of Mount Taishan. Emperor Qianlong (1711-1799) of the Qing Dynasty (1644-1911), for example, went to Mount Taishan six times in his lifetime. It was not easy for the emperors to climb more than 10 kilometers from the foot of the mountain to its peak, which usually takes about five hours. Most of them sat in sedan chairs and were carried up the mountain.

There are three gates along the mountain path, which were designed in accordance with the mountain faults. They are named the Heavenly Gate, Middle Heavenly Gate and Southern Heavenly Gate.

Daizong Archway is the entrance and also the starting point of the journey up the mountain. From the archway one has to climb a total of 6,200 stairs to reach the Southern Heavenly Gate. The slope is getting increasingly steep as one climbs up, but becomes relatively easy to scale, and then difficult again. The mountain seems to have a rhyme of its own like waves in the sea. The section from the Heavenly Gate to the Middle Heavenly Gate is the first "wave", and the rest section to the Southern Heavenly Gate, the second "wave". After passing the Southern Heavenly Gate, one reaches the top of the mountain, which is 0.6 square kilometers in area. It is a breath-taking journey for climbers, so difficult that people call it a "journey to Heaven".

From time to time, climbers can see buildings along the mountain path, where sacrificial ceremonies were held. The most important of these is the Temple of Mount Taishan, the venue of the imperial ceremony for worshipping of Earth, where the emperor would stay for the night after the ceremony. The temple used to occupy a quarter of the Tai'an City. It is in fact a palace complex — one of the three in China, the other two being the Forbidden City in Beijing and Confucius Temple in Qufu. Besides, there are also Taoist and Buddhist temples on Mount Taishan, as well as temples where folk deities are worshipped. Of these, the most many are Taoist temples.

Emperors who came are limited in numbers. In contrast, countless pilgrims, tourists and hermits have been here year after year over the past two milleniums, giving birth to Tai'an City at the foot of the mountain. Ancient people did not consider climbing a mountain an adventure, and neither did they take pleasure in conquering a mountain like we do today. In most cases, climbing a mountain was a cultural mission. Once on the mountain, they would enjoy the sight of the peaks, streams, trees and birds there with artistic concern and, inspired, many would write poems or prose. On Mount Taishan, such poems and prose can often been seen carved or painted on cliffs or rocks, and many are in fact excellent calligraphic works.

In 1987, Mount Taishan became a site of World Cultural Heritage and World Natural Heritage.

[1] Mount Taishan in Shandong Province is known as the East sacred mountain; Mount Hengshan in Hunan, as the South Sacred Mountain; Mount Huashan in Shaanxi, as the West Sacred Mountain; Mount Wutai in Shanxi, as the North Sacred Mountain; and Mount Songshan, in Henan, as the Central Sacred Mountain.

030 The most difficult section of the stairway leading to the top of Mount Taishan.

027

028

029

026 A pine tree on Mount Taishan

027 The Jade Emperor Peak of Mount Taishan. Atop the peak, one commands a full view whatever lays in an area several hundred kilometers away. Here is an old saying: "One atop Mount Taishan, everything in the whole looks small."

028 Mount Taishan shrouded in clouds.

029 Zhanlutai Crag, meaning the "crag on which to see the Kingdom of Lu". It is said that Confucius was once here to enjoy the sight of Lu, his home country.

031

031 An aerial view of Mount Taishan, to which many Chinese emperors paid tribute.

032 This stone tablet bears inscriptions of the handwriting of Emperor Xuanzong of the Tang Dynasty. He wrote these words in honor of Mount Taishan in the year 726, when he came for Heaven worshipping.

033 Evening glow seen from atop the Jade Emperor's Peak.

032

033

034

035

034 The Azure Cloud Temple on the top of the mountain, the holy shrine of the Goddess of Mount Taishan. The temple was built in the 11th century, and has undergone repeated repairs.

035 The Temple of the God of Mount Taishan at the foot of the mountain. In old times, the temple was the temporary abode of emperors who came to pay tribute to this sacred mountain.

Mausoleum of the First Qin Emperor and Terracotta Warriors

The Mausoleum of Emperor Shihuang (259-210BC) of the Qin Dynasty (221-207BC) lies at the foot of Mount Lishan 20 kilometers to the north of Xi'an, capital of Northwest China's Shaanxi Province. "Shihuang" means the "first emperor". The occupier of the mausoleum was indeed the "first". He unified China when he was 39 years old and made himself the first emperor of the Qin, China's first feudal dynasty. The dynasty, however, was short-lived. It survived for only 15 years. Historians attribute its collapse to the harsh government under his reign, to which this mausoleum may testify.

The original height of the emperor's tomb was 115 meters high, according to historical records. What we can actually see, however, is just an earthen mound. Archaeological surveys show that the mausoleum should cover an area of 56. 25 square kilometer, larger than any other imperial mausoleum in the world, and that the four sides of the area should each measure 7.5 kilometers in length. Two walls of rammed earth once surrounded the mound, the inner wall being 3, 870 meters in circumference and the outer wall, 6,321 meters. The walls are gone, but ruins of some sections and the foundations testify to their existence some 2,000 years ago.

Archeologists believe that inside the once walled mausoleum, there must be a whole array of palace halls supposedly serving the needs of the emperor in the nether world. These were exactly the same, in size and grandeur, as the halls the emperor had used before he died. Like the walls, the palace structures have all perished.

Beside the foundations of ruined walls, archeologists have found in the mausoleum area 600 pits with burial objects in them. Some pits are actually tombs, in which people were buried alive.

From one of the pits two large bronze-horse-drawn carriages have been unearthed. These are copies of the imperial traveling outfits. There are also two pits in which skeletons of hundreds of real horses were found. They were "imperial stables" in the nether world. There are also 17 pits full of skeletons of wild animals and birds, forming an imperial hunting ground. Stone armor suits were found in the largest pit discovered so far in the mausoleum area. A group of pottery acrobats were found in another pit, supposedly to entertain the dead emperor.

What merit special mention, however, are those tombs and pits in which people were buried alive. According to historical records, builders of the mausoleum in thousands were buried alive to prevent divulgence of the secret about life of the emperor in the nether world. Also buried alive were the emperor's concubines. In 17 tombs, human skeletons are found broken, with bones scattering here and there. The size of these tombs and the coffins and burial objects in them suggest that the tombs belong to the dynasty's nobles. But the gruesome scenes in the tombs lead to the guess that occupiers of the tombs could be princes who were killed in power struggles.

The emperor is buried beneath the mound, in the Underground Palace, as people call it, which is yet to be excavated.

According to historical records, the Underground Palace is extremely large in size. Its dome is painted with astronomic diagrams of jewels and precious stones. On the floor, there are imitations of rivers, lakes and seas filled with mercury in lieu of water which, driven by some mechanic device, keep flowing. There are also miniature landscapes, as well

036

as halls where the dead emperor supposedly gives imperial audience that are lit by lamps of fish oil. The underground palace is fitted with concealed weapons to kill anyone who breaks in. Back in the 1980s, scientists tested samples of soil in the mausoleum area, and found that a part of it, 12, 000 square meters large, has exceptionally high mercury content. The discovery may prove that there are rivers and lakes of the liquid metal in the Underground Palace.

Construction of the mausoleum started in 246 BC, before the "first emperor" unified China. He was then 13-years old, and had just been enthroned as king of the Qin Kingdom. As many as 700,000 people were working on the construction site during the peak of the 39-year construction. It has to be remembered that China had a population of 20 million at the time.

The most famous of all objects unearthed from the mausoleum area, are of course, those life-sized terracotta warriors and battle steeds. This terracotta army was discovered in March 1974, when some farmers were digging a well.

The terracotta warriors are in three pits, which are about five meters deep and have weight-supporting walls three meters high, and whose floors are paved with black bricks.

Pit No. 1 is the largest of the three. It is 230 meters long and 62 meters wide, covering 14,000 square meters. More than 1,000 terracotta warriors, horses and chariots have been unearthed so far. Basing themselves on the size of the pit, archeologists conclude that there should be 6,000 terracotta figures in it. These form a battle formation consisting mainly of foot soldiers. Troops in the vanguard have bows in their hands and carry arrow bags. Behind them are infantrymen wearing heavy armors. Horse-drawn chariots are also a part of the formation. The formation is protected by troops in the left and right flanks. There are also three rows of rear guards. The whole formation is well organized and looks ready for battle.

Pit No. 2 was found in April 1976 and excavation is yet to be finished. It covers 6,000 square meters. It is estimated that the pit should have 470 terracotta horses, 900 terracotta warriors, 80 wooden chariots and a large amount of metal weapons in it.

Pit No. 3 was discovered in May 1976, covering 520 square meters. So far, only a chariot and 64 terracotta soldiers have been unearthed. Archaeologists agree that the figures found in the pit form the command headquarters of the whole terracotta army.

Archeologists are expecting to find 7,000 terracotta soldiers, 600 terracotta horses, 100 or so chariots and several thousands weapons when excavation of all the three pits is completed. The highest terracotta figurine stands nearly 2 meters high and the shortest, 1.7 meters. The average height is 1.8 meters. They have different features, postures and facial expressions. Not a single figurine repeats the other in this regard. Each figurine was modeled on a real man. Everything in the terracotta warrior is meticulously done — physical structure, hair, eyebrows, shoes and even the needlework on shoelaces. The terracotta horses are 1.5 meters high and two meters long on an average.

The terracotta figurines were produced roughly through the following process:

The first step was to make clay roughcasts, which were then covered with a layer of fine mud on which facial expressions and other details were carved. When the roughcasts became dry and hardened, they were baked in a kiln. The last step was to paint the baked figurines. When unearthed, many figurines were broken and virtually all were discolored as a result of exposure to moisture over the past two milleniums.

Thousands of weapons have been unearthed from the pits, mostly of bronze and tin. They look brand new, without rust. Tests show that the weapon pieces are covered with a layer of chrome salt oxide substance. Modern chrome electroplating technology was patented in Germany and the United States in 1937 and 1950, respectively. There are no historical records about how the Qin artisans mastered the technology.

The terracotta army is only the tip of the iceberg. Archaeologists say that the mausoleum is so great that it may take 200 more years to get to know it thoroughly.

In 1987, the Mausoleum was listed as a site of World's Cultural Heritage.

036 The Mausoleum of the Qin Emperor Shihuang was designed to cover 56 square kilometers. Today we find only an earthen mound. All other structures on the ground were gone due to erosion of weather over the past 2, 000 years.

037 Photo shows Pit No. 1, which is 5 meters deep and has a weight-supporting wall every three meters. Some 1,000 terracotta warriors, horses and chariots have been unearthed from the pit.

037

041 ▶

038

039

040

038 Colored pottery horses excavated from Pit No 1. These average 1.5 meters tall and 2 meters long.

039 Photo shows the back of a terracotta general.

040 Photo shows two of the terracotta court officials found in a funerary pit at the site of the mausoleum. Twelve colored terracotta figurines were unearthed from the pit in 2002, which are 1.9 meters tall on an average.

041 The terracotta general unearthed from Pit No 1. It is 1.9 meters tall. Pay attention to his headgear and double-layer robe, which distinguishes him from the rank-and-file.

043

042 Shown here is a soldier ready to shoot, which was unearthed from Pit No. 2.

043 Photo shows one of the two bronze horse chariots unearthed in 1980. The painted chariots are decorated with a large amount of gold and silver pieces. With 7,000 parts and accessories, the chariots have a combined weight of 2.3 tons.

044 The other bronze horse chariot.

◄ 042

044

045

046

045 Pit No. 3 covers 520 square meters. It is the commanding post of the "imperial army".

046 Many colored figurines were broken and discolored when they were unearthed. However, the vast majority had remnants of the original colors, and colors on some were largely intact.

047 The Stone Armor Pit is the largest funerary pit found at the site of the mausoleum so far. Shown here is a set of stone armor.

048 Photo shows a bronze tripod unearthed from Pit No. 5 in 1999. It is 60 centimeters high and weighs 212 kilograms, the largest of its kind unearthed so far.

049 One of the parts of a bronze horse chariot is shown in this picture. It is used to extend the rod of the canopy.

050 The bronze bell unearthed from Pit No. 1 is for directing the troops in combat.

047

048

049

050

The Mogao Caves

One evening in the year 366, Le Zun, a Buddhist monk, was traveling across Mount Sanwei in Northwest China's Dunhuang when, suddenly, he saw golden light rays atop the mountain. Taking for granted that Buddhist deities were making appearances there, he cut short his travel and began digging a grotto for himself to practice Buddhism in. This marked the beginning of the construction of the Muogao Grotto in Dunhuang's Mingsha Hills.

Dunhuang was a hub on the ancient Silk Road, via which Buddhism found its way into China 2,000 years ago. Central Asian, West Asian and even European merchants, envoys and monks kept traveling through the area, leaving behind stamps of their own cultures and faiths. Dunhuang was a prosperous place at the time, evidenced in its name: "Dun" meaning "big", and "Huang", "prosperity".

Building of grottoes and Buddha figures lasted 1,000 years after Monk Lezun's initial act and began to decline from the 14th century.

There are now more than 700 stone grottoes on five planes in the Mogao Grottoes area, which are densely aligned along the 1,600-meter cliffs. The biggest covers 268 square meters and the smallest can only be large enough for a hat. The highest stands about 50 meters. There are altogether 45, 000 square meters of murals and 2,400 colorful sculptures in 492 caves. The whole area is regarded as the greatest treasure trove of Buddhist art in the world.

Buddhism in China peaked in the Sui (581-618) and Tang (618-907) dynasties. The period naturally marked the zenith of the Mogao Grottoes.

Numerous ethnic groups lived in the area in a time span of 1,000 years and at the same time, the Chinese, Indian, Islam and Greek cultures interacted to each other here. Each ethnic group, each culture and each historical period have more or less left their influence.

The murals are the quintessence of the art in the Mogao Grottoes. The rich content involves Buddhist tales, paintings based on Buddhist scripts, Buddhist figures, sacrifice providers and decorative patterns. Of these, pieces done during the Sui and Tang periods make up more than one-half. Peeling walls, however, reveal a little secret: later paintings cover the earlier layer upon layer. In some sections, there are four or five layers of murals.

Styles and themes vary from period to period. The Sui Dynasty is a watershed, when paintings based on Buddhist tales depicting practice of Buddhism in a painstaking way and advancing morally through utmost forbearance were yielding place to individual Bodhisattva figures and paintings based on Buddhist script. Murals on the ceilings of the grottoes, which often advocate one could become Buddha simply through one's faith or depict the Buddhist paradise, were making their way to the grotto walls. In early murals, Bodhisattva was always a secondary figure beside the Buddha. The debut of individual Bodhisattva as independent figures in the Sui murals marked the beginning of localization of Buddhism in China. Costumes and decorations in the murals of this period became elaborately beautiful, more heart warming, full of human touch and more meticulous.

The artistic enthusiasm, which was an expression of the prosperity of the Tan Dynasty at its peak, found expression in full-wall murals based on Buddhist scripts. In one such mural, there could be more than 1,000 figures. The artists' daring and their skills to handle complicated composition conquer the posterity viewers. In these paintings, all possible colors in this world explode but are at the same time well controlled, forming color patches outlined by fluent lines. Birds and animals are dancing and clusters of flowers form patterns. Buddhist deities have vivid facial ions and

051

are exuberant. They are unlike the murals found in the heartland of China. The latter are often implicit and serious-looking.

In the post-Tang period, the artistic enthusiasm continucd, but a bit moderated. Wilderness was yielding to coolness and the ways of expression became more meticulous. The passion, however, had become subsided by the Song Dynasty. Dancing postures of the mural figures became self-conscious. Although excellent expression was found here and there, the exuberant and joyful atmosphere as a whole was gone.

The Tang culture in general kindled the brilliant flame of the Dunhuang Buddhist arts. The murals turn the reality into ideal and vice versa. Free artistic creation makes the Buddha a figure living in this world and renders Bodhisattva as a loving woman. All this makes the realm of Buddhism secular and full of humanity and vigor. All kinds of patterns outlined by fluently curved lines add a strong sense of movement and make the pictures colorful.

In portraying religious themes, some scenes of secular life are intentionally or unintentionally incorporated into the murals. Different ways of life and working, different customs, dances, music and costumes in different periods that spanned 1,000 years are seen in the murals.

Colorful sculptures in the grottoes rival the murals in magnificence. The Dunhuang grottoes are carved out of the rocks, which makes it impossible for meticulous stone sculptures. So, traditional Chinese clay sculpture techniques were widely applied from the very beginning. The clay sculptures were then painted with colors. The sculptural pieces can be classified into four categories: Buddha figures, Bodhisattva figures, disciple figures and deities. Large-scale sculptural pieces are often alone. The highest piece stands 34.5 meters high and the smallest only two centimeters. Figures of some secular people are occasionally among the divine ones.

Colored sculptures have different styles in different periods. Early ones have vivid facial expressions to the neglect of body depiction. They have generally simple colors, look solemn and cool, reflecting influences of Indian and Central Asian cultures. At the same time, influence of the indigenous Chinese culture is also obvious, which emphasizes underlying spirit.

Colored sculptures wrought in the Sui Dynasty excel in both sculpturing and painting skills. Colors are getting increasingly rich. However, compared with the pieces of the Tang Dynasty, the Sui pieces have distinct transitory features.

Of the 2,400 colored sculptures in the Mogao Grottoes, those made during the Tang Dynasty roughly make up one-half. Besides group sculptures, the two largest sculptures are Tang pieces. The Tang sculptures are splendidly wrought, with rich colors. The figures look dignified while showing secular desires. They are realist figures, with proper human-body proportions and the configurations are outlined by smooth and fluent lines. The psychology and characters of the figures are especially well depicted.

Colored sculpturcs distinctly declined after the Tang Dynasty, which is evidenced in the pieces wrought in the following times. These pieces are mostly stereotyped and have dumb expressions. This can be explained by the fact that people in the periods following the Tang Dynasty were much less enthusiastic about creating Buddhist figures than their predecessors in the Tang period. Moreover, few of these relatively inferior sculptures have survived the times because they were mostly placed close to the ground.

The most important of all the grottoes at Dunhuang is No. 17 Grotto, or the Script Storage Grotto.

A Taoist priest happened to discover a small cave, which

had been closed for centuries, when he was clearing piled up sand on June 22, 1900. In the grotto there were stockpiled documents, scripts, silk paintings, instruments for Buddhist rituals and so on, 50,000 pieces in all. Buddhist scripts accounted for the better part of the documents and scripts. In addition, there were historical, geographic and astronomic records. Accounting books and books of poems and local customs were also found in the grotto. These were products of the historical period spanning the 4th century and the 11th century. They were missing historical materials or rarely seen ones. Most of the documents and scripts were written in Chinese characters. Some are in ethnic minority groups' scripts or in foreign words.

Who stored all these in the cave? When? And Why? The questions remain unanswered up till now. And, who shut up the cave entrance and covered it with murals? This is another question yet to be answered. Are there any other script grottoes in the area? Nobody knows for sure.

The news soon spread across the world. Adventurers and scholars soon came to Dunhuang from Britain, France, the United States, Russia and Japan. Ungracefully, they transported many valuable relics out of China.

The discovery of the Script Storage Grotto made Dunhuang known to the world. The scripts found there gave rise to a new branch of learning: Dunhuang studies. At first, Dunhuang studies focused on the scripts and documents found in the Script Storage Grotto and later extended to issues related to the Script Storage Grotto and further to research on Dunhuang grottoes as a whole and the culture and history of Dunhuang. The academic learning eventually came to cover geography, history, archaeology, arts, religion, literature, language, local customs, ancient science and technology, document studies, grotto protection and so on.

In 1987, the Mogao Grottoes was listed as the World' s Cultural Heritage.

051 This Bodhisattva statue enshrined in Cave No. 384 features a realist style that characterizes sculptures produced during the Tang Dynasty.

052 A full view of the site of the Mogao Grottoes.

052

053 The mural, found in the Scripture Storage Cave, depicts the soul of a dead woman being led to paradise by a Buddhist goddess.

054 The North Wei (386-534) colored clay sculpture of Buddha enshrined in Cave No. 259. Pay attention to his gentle smile.

055 Cave No. 17, or the "Scripture Storage Cave", had remained closed for centuries until it was opened by chance in 1900. Documents, paintings and sacrificial instruments, 50,000 pieces in all, were found in it.

056 A hand-written astrology book was found in the Scripture Storage Cave. Shown here is a page of the book.

054

055

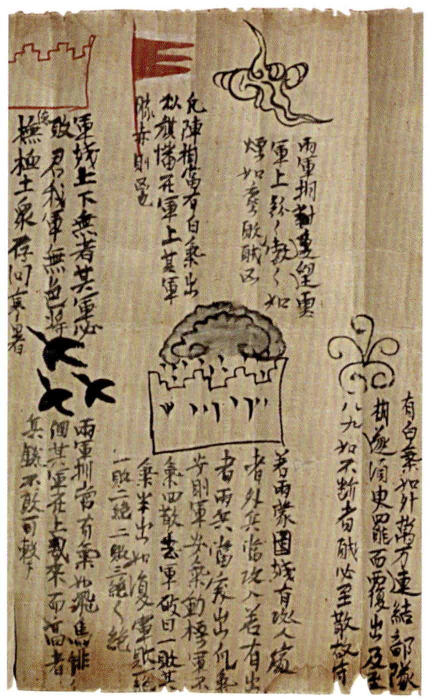

056

057 A Bodhisattva statue left over from the Tang Dynasty, which is enshrined in Cave No. 194. It is plump in shape and wears high hair buns and thin garments, reflecting the aesthetic taste prevalent at the time.

058 This cross-legged Bodhisattva enshrined in Cave No. 275 was made in 5th century, from which a strong influence of the Indian culture can clearly be seen.

059

058

059 A Chinese deity on a Sui Dynasty (581-618) mural found in Cave No. 423. Pay attention to the fluent lines.

060 A group of Buddhist figures on a mural found in Cave No. 285, which was built during the North Wei Dynasty (535-556). The imported technique of ink-splashing is used on the mural.

◄ *057*

060

061

062

061 This mural in Cave No. 103 is based on a story told in Buddhist classics, about a saint named Vimalakirti debating with Bodhisattva on some Buddhist teachings. Vimalakirti, so goes the story, pretends to be ill in order to have Bodhisattva with him for the debate.

062 This mural in Cave No. 296 brings back to life the ancient Silk Road. It was produced during the North Zhou Dynasty (557-581).

063 The paradise as perceived by Buddhists is depicted in vivid details on this mural in Cave No. 217.

063

Peking Man Site at Zhoukoudian

Zhoukoudian, home to Peking Man, is a small rural town some 50 kilometers to the southwest of Beijing. On the Dragon Bone Hill near the town, there is a natural cave 140 meters long and 2.5 - 42 meters wide, where Peking Man was found.

No one knows when local people began digging on the hill in search of "dragon bones", which they sold as a traditional medicinal material. The so-called "dragon bones" are in fact mammal fossil fragments. Neither anybody knows how the place became known in the early 20th century for possible scientific value to foreign scientists.

Austrian paleontologist Otto Zdansky and Swedish geologist J. Gunnar Anderson were among the first to come. Through trial excavation on the Dragon Bone Hill in 1921, the pair found some animal fossils and quartz fragments sharpened like knife blades. According to their published diary, Anderson once told Zdansky: "I have the foreboding that Man's ancestor sleeps here."

To be more precise, they obtained two molar teeth in 1921 and 1923, respectively, but had no idea of what the teeth were at the time. By 1926, however, the scientists had identified it as a hominid teeth and made their discovery public.

The following year, a scientific expedition team of Chinese and foreign scientists came, and excavation began on full scale on the Dragon Bone Hill. The same year, they found a hominid tooth in perfect conditions, and named its owner Sinanthropus pekinensis, meaning the "Peking species of the Chinese ape-man" in plain language. Not long afterwards, the name was changed into Homoerectus pekinensis, meaning "Peking Man erectus", or "Peking Man" for short.

On December 2, 1929, Pei Wenzhong, a Chinese scientist in charge of the fieldwork, found a Homo erectus skullcap in a cave on the Dragon Bone Hill, the very first of its kind ever discovered in the world. Before long, the discovery became known across the world.

More were to be found in the same cave — stone and bone artifacts as well the evidence to use of fire by the Homo erectus who once lived in the cave. The Dragon Bone Hill, the cave on it in particular, naturally aroused the attention of the global science community as an important hominid site.

In 11 days in November 1936, three more Homo erectus skullcaps were excavated in succession from the same layer in the same cave on the Dragon Bone Hill. The excavation had to stop the following year when the War of Resistance against Japanese Aggression broke out. At the end of November 1941, all the four skullcaps disappeared from Beijing, which was then under Japanese occupation, along with other specimens collected from the Dragon Bone Hill, and their whereabouts have remained unknown. The sole Homo erectus skullcap displayed at the Peking Man Museum at Zhoukoudian comprises fragmented skullcap fossils found separately, which are pieced together for exhibition.

Excavation resumed soon after the People's Republic of China was founded in October 1949. Fragmented facial and limb bones and teeth have been discovered over the past decades, which scientists identify as belonging to more than 40 members of the Peking Man family. Also found are more than 100,000 finished or semi-finished stone tools, along with numerous bone and horn artifacts and fossils of more than 100 animal species, as well as more evidence to use of fire by Peking Man.

064

The site of Peking Man has provided scientific evidence to research into the origin and evolution of the human being.

Dutch scientist Eugene Dubois discovered a hominid skullcap in Indonesia in 1891, its owner known as "Homo erectus" to scientist or "Java Man" to the layman. However, scientists at the time were divided on what the fossil actually was, on whether it belonged to Man or the ape. Without further evidence, Dubois changed his mind in the end, claiming that Java Man may have nothing to do with the evolution of Man. Peking Man, however, was soon accepted by the world science community as Man's ancestor, and the recognition brought the debate on Java Man to an end.

Peking Man, a species of Homo erectus, represents an important link in the evolution of the human being, the process of the ape becoming Man. Fossils of the same kind have been discovered elsewhere in the world. Despite that, the Peking Man site remains one of the most important as it harbors the most complete, most abundant evidence to this evolution.

The Peking Man cave has an accumulation about 40 meters thick, with 13 fossil-containing layers. These layers were formed less than half a million years ago, the result of caves-in and discarding of garbage by Peking Man. Before Peking Man came to dwell, the cave had been occupied more than once by the Chinese hyena. The animal, already extinct, had the habit of leaving its dropping in a fixed place, and such droppings have been found in some of the layers.

It is generally agreed that Peking Man came to live in the cave somewhere between 500,000 to 200,000 years ago, though some scientists put the period even earlier, to 700, 000 years ago. But the ape-like human being came in separate groups, not as one group who came to live in the cave continuously, generation after generation. Scientists base this conclusion on the fact that no trace of human culture has been found in layers with hyena droppings. It is assumed that one group of the Peking Man family may have lived here for a period, and then left for shortage of food or severe weather. Then another group of Peking Man came many years later.

Paleontologists say that half of the Peking Man family was unable to live longer than 14 years. Peking Man's cerebral volume was about 80 percent as large as that of modern Man, but it was much larger than that of the ape. The cerebral volume of the modern ape is 60 percent smaller than that of Peking Man. Peking Man's upper limbs were was already developed enough to do some kind of labor with the hands. The lower limbs had a lot in common with Man's, but the knees were a bit too bent. Despite that, scientists believe that Peking Man was able to stand erect and walk. In the cave of Peking Man, four layers of ashes have been discovered, along with burned bone fragments and charcoal. This proves that Peking Man had already learned to use fire for roasting games meet and keeping warm against cold. Of course, they only used natural fire - fire ignited by lightning, for example, but they knew how to keep live cinders for starting new fires with.

Peking Man vanished about 200,000 years ago. It is still unclear where they had come from and where they headed for after leaving the cave on the Dragon Bone Hill.

In a cave near the top of the Dragon Bone Hill, above the Peking Man site, scientists found, in 1933, some complete hominid skullcaps and skull fragments identified as belonging to at least seven or eight individuals of the "Upper Cave Man" family. Red iron ore powder was found round the bones, suggesting that Upper Cave Man already may have developed something like a funeral. Also found in the cave are bone needles, bone pendants with holes and "necklaces" of fish bone and animal teeth. It seems that Upper Cave Man was able to sew pieces of animal skin together for "clothing" and produce personal ornaments. Upper Cave Man lived 180,000 years ago. Scientists have concluded that Upper Cave Man was not the descendent of Peking Man.

In 1987, the Peking Man site at Zhoukoudian was inscribed on the UNESCO list of World Cultural Heritage.

067 The natural cave in Dragon Bone Hill at Zhoukoudian, where the first skullcap of Peking Man was found on December 2, 1929.

065

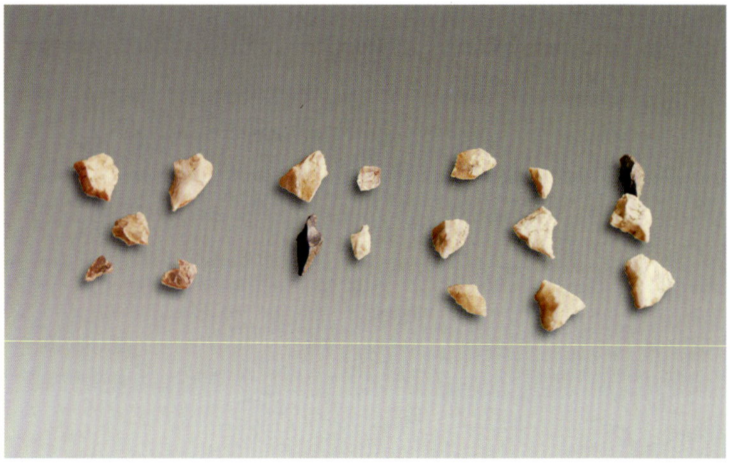

066

064 An artist perception of Peking Man using fire.

065 Peking Man.

066 As many as 100,000 stone artifacts have been unearthed at the site of Peking Man, which can be used for chopping, striking, scraping and piercing.

067 ►

猿人洞

068

069

070

068 Five Peking Man skullcaps disappeared in 1941 when transported elsewhere for safekeeping. These are their replicas.

069 Excavation being done at the Peking Man site in 1927.

070 The first Peking Man skullcap restored and packed with gypsum. The man holding the skullcap is Pei Wenzhong who found it.

071

071 In a cave on the top of the Dragon Bone Hill, fossils of Upper Cave Man that lived 18,000 years ago were discovered in 1933. These fossils led to restoration of Upper Cave Man's image.

072 A "necklace" of animal bones and teeth, shells and stone bids possibly used as a personal ornament by Upper Cave Man.

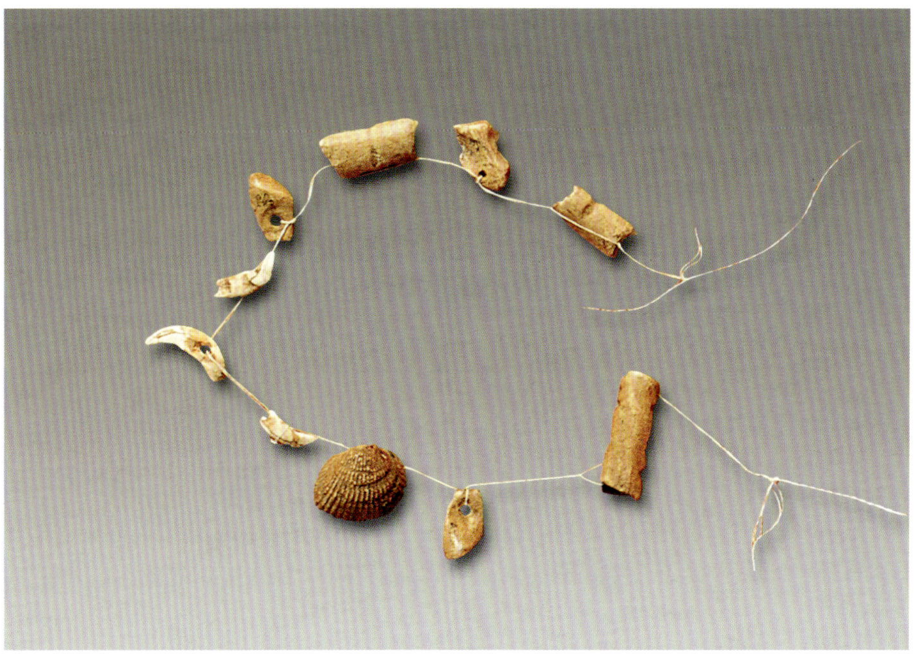

072

Mount Huangshan

To enjoy the magnificence of a mountain, you have to look upward in most cases. To enjoy the magnificence of Mount Huangshan, however, you've got to look downward. In this 154 square kilometer-scenic area in south Anhui Province, there are 77 peaks. Once on top of any of these peaks, you will have a bird's-eye-view of cluster upon cluster of peaks rising in the distance from beneath a sea of clouds. These appear so close to one another that you'll actually see a forest of peaks.

The Lotus Peak, 1,862 meters above sea level, is the highest of all peaks. It is thus called because it looks like a blossoming lotus flower. The Guangming Peak, the second highest, rises 1,841 meters above sea level, which has a flat top — ideal for watching the rising sun and the boundless sea of clouds below. An old saying goes like this: You'll miss the scenic beauty of Mt. Huangshan without climbing to the top of the Guangming Peak. The third highest peak is called Tiandu, which means "heavenly capital". Though not as high as Lotus and Guangming, it is however most imposing and steep. The Tiandu Peak epitomizes wonders of Mount Huangshan and is called "the best" of the peaks. A dozen peaks, including the three highest, are open to climbers. The other peaks are simply inaccessible.

On all these peaks you'll find rocks in exotic shapes. A large rock may look like a precipitous cliff, and a small rock, like a tree in miniature. There are also rocks that look like human figures or animals. Some do not look like any real thing, but they are beautiful all the same with looks so grotesque in shape as to beggar description.

When you're atop one of these peaks, don't forget to look around. Peaks or rocks in the distance would present different views when viewed from different directions. When looking at the Tiandu Peak from Yuping Peak, you see something like a squirrel on a neighboring peak ready to jump to the Tiandu Peak. The "squirrel", so to speak, is a rock. Once you are atop the Tiandu Peak, the same rock looks just like an odd shoe.

Pine trees in Mount Huangshan cliffs are no less beautiful than those rocks. Most pine trees here grow in places that rise at least 800 meters above sea level and are often rooted in crevices of granite rocks hardly with any soil. Moreover, they vary in height. The highest can be several dozen meters high, and the shortest may just be 10 or 20 centimeters. Their trunks and branches are crooked and their crowns are often flat. By Chinese aesthetic standards, the more crooked a plant is, the more beautiful will it be. Strange shapes, as a matter of fact, constitute one salient feature for pine trees in Mount Huangshan.

Why is it that pine trees can grow in crevices of granite rocks? This has something to do with the root system of the tree. The roots of pine trees in Mount Huangshan can secrete a kind of organic acid, which together with the carbon dioxide released from the roots, forms a kind of carbonic acid when meeting with water. The carbonic acid slowly melts the rock and helps the tree roots to get nutrition and water from the rock. As a result, the roots go down deeper and deeper. In general, the root of a pine tree can be several times the height of the tree itself. In addition, pine trees here are good at protecting themselves. Their needles are exceptionally short and hard, and this helps reduce evaporation of the precious moisture.

Pine trees grow extremely slowly because of harsh natural conditions. Even though small, a pine tree may be several hundred years old. However, they never wither and are

073

obstinate against strong wind and heavy snow. The higher the mountain peak is, the greener are the trees there. Back in the 1930s, botanists identified pine trees in Mount Huangshan as of an independent pine species, which they named after Mount Huangshan. For its tenacity and vitality in resisting natural adversities, the Mount Huangshan pine is seen as a symbol of willpower and has been chosen as the logo of Anhui Province.

In about 250 days in a year, clouds add to the beauty and magnificence of Mount Huangshan. When the clouds are thick, peaks in the distance will look like isles on the turbulent sea. Looking around, you find that far, far away, probably several hundred kilometers away, clouds converge round peaks, forming an ocean that seems to engulf the world. The sea of clouds inspired ancient Chinese to call Mount Huangshan the "Huangshan Sea". The names of many scenic spots in the area are associated with the sea — the "South Sea", "North Sea", etc.

The sea of clouds appears in Mount Huangshan on an average of 52 times a year. The best time to view the sea of clouds is from November to April of the following year. Sometimes, the sea of clouds appears at sunrise or sundown. If you're lucky enough to be there, you'll see a sea of rosy clouds.

Peaks, rocks, pine trees and clouds together form scenes with a strong enough visual impact to give loose to people's imaginations, hence those poetic — if not strange — names given to scenic spots in Mount Huangshan. Just to name a few: the Tiandu (heavenly capital) Peak, Buddha's Palm Peak, Xianrenzhilu (god showing the way) peak, and the Peak of Old Man Picking Herbs. Some scenes are named after their shapes, such as the Lotus Peak, Qintai Peak (platform for the traditional Chinese plucked instrument called "*qin*"), Fan-shaped Pine Tree, etc. Some names contain both people's imagination and feelings: Farming in the Cloud Peak, Old Man Fishing Peak, and Guest Greeting Pine. Some of the names have historical stories or folk tales behind them. Viewers with different cultural backgrounds may have different imaginations when looking at the same scene. No wonder some say Mount Huangshan is a "great garden of folk culture."

Strange-looking pine trees, grotesque rocks and the sea of clouds are the most enchanting scenes Mount Huangshan is able to present. Once upon a time, a man did not believe in this. He made up his mind to go to Mount Huangshan himself to see whether the mountain was really as beautiful as it had been said. After he visited just a few of the peaks, he became convinced that Mount Huangshan was really as beautiful as it had been described. One of the peaks was thus named as "Shixin", literally "one is convinced only after one comes and sees for oneself".

Mount Huangshan is unique in many ways. An old saying goes like this: "Other mountains stand out with their different shapes, which one can see with one's own eyes. But scenery in Mount Huangshan changes constantly, and one can never see enough of it."

Probably for this reason, Mount Huangshan has beggared the Chinese language. Those who proved excellent in writing about other mountains often felt at a loss about what to do with this mountain, and some even gave up writing about it. More than 20,000 poems and essays have been written about Mount Huangshan since ancient times, and none is good enough to be a masterpiece. But these lines from an essay have been frequently quoted: "No mountain can match

Mount Huangshan in beauty. Once on top of Mount Huangshan, one instantly becomes apathetic towards all other mountains!"

However, Mount Huangshan has always been a favorite for ancient Chinese literati landscape painters. Mountain peaks, the sea of clouds, strange-looking pine trees and grotesque rocks these were living things in their mind's eye, something that were good enough to reflect their proud inner world. Many famous mountains and valleys were subjects under the painting brushes, but Mount Huangshan was always the most favored subject in traditional Chinese landscape painting. Of the various schools of traditional Chinese painting, only one school is named after a mountain, and that mountain is none other than Mount Huangshan. Jian Jiang (1610-1664), Mei Qing (1623-1679) and Shi Tao (1642-c 1718) have been known as the best painters of this school. Shi Tao once said: "Mount Huangshan is my teacher, and I am Mount Huangshan's friend."

In May 1990, a group of experts from the UNESCO made an inspection tour of Mount Huangshan. In June, the experts asked the Chinese side to get Mount Huangshan listed as a site of both natural and cultural heritage for the world. It is only by then had the Chinese side realized that they had underestimated the value of Mount Huangshan.

074

075

073 The Guest-Welcoming Pine on the eastern slope of Jade Screen Peak, the landmark of Mount Huangshan.

074 A forest of peaks in the sea of clouds.

075 Tiandu Peak, or the Peak of Heavenly Capital.

076

076 A photo or a traditional Chinese painting ? The peak in the background is the Peak of Heavenly Capital.

079

077 Strange-looking pine trees, grotesque rocks and the sea of clouds are three most fantastic scenes on Mount Huangshan.

078 Rolling peaks in the Mount Huangshan scenic area.

080

081

082

079 An ocean of clouds.

080 Pine trees on Mount Huangshan, which features a unique beauty with crooked trunks and branches and flat crowns.

081 "Buddha's halos" often appear two or three hours after sunrise or before sunset.

082 The Western Sea Canyon.

Jiuzhaigou Valley Scenic and Historic Interest Area

Here we are at Jiuzhaigou in the northwest of Sichuan Province, southwest China, the "fairyland" or the "world in fairy tales" as it is known in China and the rest of the world.

With an area of 720 square kilometers, the Jiuzhaigou scenic area lies deep in mountains which, covered by lush-green forests, rise from 2,000 meters above sea level to 4, 764 meters. The main gully in the area is 50 kilometers long. The section down the slope called Shuzhen Gully which, at 14 kilometers up, splits into two gullies, Rize and Zechawa. Nine Tibetan villages are counted in these gullies, hence the name of the place "Nine Village Gully" or Jiuzhaigou.

The area had been almost completely inaccessible to the outside world until it was discovered by a group of lumberjacks. In 1978, the area was designated a nature reserve. On December 5, 1992, it was put on the UNESCO list of World Natural Heritage.

Crystal clean ponds, waterfalls, forests, snow-clad mountain peaks and Tibetan folk culture are the major attractions in the area. What merits special mention, however, are the ponds and waterfalls.

Upon entering the gully, you'll find yourself in a world of lush green and tranquility, a fictitious land of peace. Those ponds look so mysterious and sacred that instantly, you'll feel completely free from this earthly world. Down the slope with a fall of 1,800 meters, 114 ponds are counted on different heights. Water flows from the ponds are so gentle, and so quiet, that ripples are hardly discernible. Water here is so pure, and so transparent, that you can clear see those pure white rocks and green weeds on the bottom of a pond several dozen meters deep. As the saying goes, "when water is too pure, no fish can survive in it." In Jiuzhaigou ponds, the only fish you can find is a species tiny in size and without scales.

The gully has 17 groups of waterfalls, which fall through a number of terraces, thus forming different layers of waterfalls. Almost all waterfalls originate from forests up the mountains, presenting a picture of "trees in water and water flowing through trees". The Nuorilang Waterfall, 2, 365 meters above sea level, 30 meters high and 270 meters wide, is the greatest in the gully. It is the landmark of the Jiuzhaigou scenic area.

Water is the soul of Jiuzhaigou. What is unique is that water surfaces here can be colorful like rainbows. Geologists believe that ponds at the Jiuzhaigou were created by glacier movements that blocked water flows at the entrance of the gully. Mud-and-rock flows and landslides have also created ponds. The Changhai Pond is the largest of all the ponds in the gully. The pond, which lies 3,102 meters above

083

sea level, is seven kilometers long and 80 meters deep. It collects water of melted snow and springs. Without an outlet, it depends on evaporation and under currents for drainage. The pond never overflows even in heaviest rains and never dries up even in severest drought. It freezes in winter and loud sound can be heard from beneath the ice. Legend goes that the sound is produced by dragons living in the pond.

Water here is rich in calcium carbonate and, as water overflows, calcium carbonate is released. Through a slow, elaborate process of chemical reactions, deposits of travertine are formed and keep settling on the ponds' beds and banks. Travertine "dikes" are thus formed. As water flows over the "dikes", waterfalls and cascades are created.

Here is a string of ponds called "Shuzhengqun". Consisting of 19 ponds, the string is five kilometers long, with a drop of about 100 meters. The smallest ponds are only a few dozen square meters large, and the largest, more than 1,000 square meters. The terraces, the ponds as well, are not far from each other, as if they are strung like a string of pearls. The travertine "dikes" vary in height, ranging from less than one to several meters. Willow, pine, cypress and fir trees grow luxuriantly beyond those creamy "dikes".

Reeds and weeds grow in shallow waters, where bunches of bushes are surrounded by deposit of travertine, presenting miniature landscapes or "potted landscape shoals".

In relatively flat places, travertine would deposit in layers if ponds there are not deep, thus forming travertine shoals with a surface of many breast-shaped bulging parts. The Pearl Shoal is the most typical, which is 189 meters long and 112 meter wide. Water is quite shallow here, and breast-shaped bulging parts in the water make it look like a string of pearls.

As travertine dikes becomes higher and higher in lower parts of the gully, the water level will be raised, causing flooding of travertine dikes upstream. The Crouching Dragon Pond is a case in point. The pond, 2,215 meters above sea level, 22 meters deep and with area of 60,000 square meters, has a creamy travertine dike lying on its bed, which looks like a dragon sleeping there.

Dead plants in ponds never decay because water is cold and, moreover, dead plants are wrapped in travertine and algae. The fantastic scenes and colors of the ponds here are beyond people's imagination. These pose a challenge to painters but are a gift to photographers. Let's see the Pond of Five Flowers, which lies 2,472 meters above sea level, is five meters deep and has a water surface of 90,000 square meters. Several colors make up the water surface - lush green, azure blue, deep purple, orange red and golden yellow. Experts believe the different colors should have something to do with geological structure, deposits, depth of water, algae in the water and clouds in the sky as well.

The forests are also colorful. Virgin forests can be spotted in half of the area in the gully. Because of the different altitude and vertical change of climate at different altitude, forests at different heights are in different colors — green down the slope, then yellow a few kilometers up, and finally white.

The gully is covered with snow for six months in a year, usually from October to April of the following year, during which ponds will be frozen entirely or partially and waterfalls will stop flowing and turn into sculptures of ice.

Wild animals found in the forests fall into 170 species, birds, 141, and plants, nearly 3,000. Jiuzhaigou is a natural habitat of the giant panda, one of the rarest species in the world.

083 Dead plants in water at Jiuzhaigou never decay.

084 The scenery changes at Jiuzhaigou with the change of seasons.

085 The Pond of Sparks. The "sparks", so to speak, are those dazzling ripples that keep dancing under the sun.

086 The Pond of Grass.

084

085

086

◄ 087

088

087 The Swan Pond.

088 So tranquil and peaceful? a glimpse of a gully at Jiuzhaigou.

089 Ponds at different heights. At Jiuzhaigou, altogether 114 plateau ponds are counted.

090 The Five-Color Pond. The pond is thus called because different parts of its water surface have different colors, and these colors will instantly change when water in the pond is stirred by wind.

091 A glimpse of the Changhai Pond, the largest water body at Jiuzhaigou. The pond, seven kilometers long and 80 meters deep, collects water of springs and thawing snow. It never overflows even in a heaviest rain and never dries up even in a severest drought.

092 Nuorilang waterfall, a landmark for Jiuzhaigou.

089

090

Wulingyuan Scenic and Historic Interest Area

The mountainous Wuliangyuan area had remained obscure until the 1970s when some painters and photographers happened to come, and were amazed by its surpassing beauty and magnificence. Before long, the area became known across the country and, in 1992, was inscribed on the UNESCO list of World Natural Heritage. A report of the UNESCO World Heritage Committee describes the area as "spectacular". Stretching more than 200 kilometers in Central China's Hunan Province, the report says, the site is dominated by more than 3,000 narrow sandstone pillars and peaks, many over 200 meters high. Between the peaks lie ravines and gorges with streams, pools and waterfalls, some 40 caves, and two large natural bridges. In addition to the striking beauty of the landscape, the region is also noted as home to some endangered plant and animal species.

The Wulingyuan area encompasses the Zhangjiajie National Forest Park, Suoxiyu Nature Reserve, Tianzishan Nature Reserve and Yangjiajie Nature Reserve, which are all under state-level protection. Most parts of this area are sparsely populated and still maintain their original features.

A mountain normally has one peak or a few. Wulingyuan, however, boasts a forest of peaks. Most mountains have a slope, making it possible for people to climb the top. But peaks in Wulingyuan are in fact precipitous cliffs, their slopes strewn with sharp edges that make climbing almost impossible.

Surrounded by rock walls, the forest of peaks, when looked from afar, is quite like an area of small hills. But upon entering the scenic spot, we have in front of us a deep, tranquil world with stunning beauty. The heights of the peaks vary from a few dozen meters to some 400. Most peaks look like pillars or awls chopped out with a knife or an ax. Some peaks have their tops larger then their feet and look as if they were weightless and floating in the air. Some tilt or hang in the air as if they would crush at any time. Some have big cracks from their feet to their tops. None of them look the same, but all of them have a platform on the top, where several trees or even a forest grow. The trees are green all the year round and, in shape, are as exotic as the rock peaks.

As if in a grand party or a mass march, the 3,103 peaks stand there in their own postures which, because of a sudden change, have stopped there for good. A vast ocean used to be here 300 million years ago, according to geologists. The ocean receded, and out came the sedimentary rocks, which finally turned into today's rock pillars, peaks, cliffs, stone bridges or doors after having been washed, cut and eroded by water, wind and organisms in millions of years. There are still sedimentary lines of seawater and traces of wave erosion on some rocks today. There are also coral fossils, which look quite like the backs of turtles.

Mountain peaks in Wulingyuan are primarily made of quartzose sandstone. There are also limestone and arenaceous rocks. Quartzose sandstone and arenaceous rocks alternate each other to form different layers, the former is thick and the latter thin, and it seems as if they were laid artificially.

093

The lines of different layers are very explicit to give out the gradation. Since the quartzose sandstone is strongly resistant to erosion, many rock pillars have stood there for many milleniums without falling down although their heads are bigger than their feet. The rigid quartzose sandstone will fall apart or sink in full lumps. Therefore, the rock peaks here seldom have curved sides and just present straight lines as if they were chopped or cut by knifes vertically, horizontally or slantingly.

Of all the scenic spots in Wulingyuan, Zhangjiajie is the most famous. Huangshizhai is the highest peak of all peaks in Zhangjiajie, and on top of the peak is a natural sightseeing platform. Looking from the peak top, one can see nothing but peaks and forests. The locals say that one would have made a fruitless trip to Zhangjiajie without climbing up onto Huangshizhai Peak. However, some argue that one can never have a better understanding of Wulingyuan without making a trip to the forest park on Mount Tianzishan, which is in a comparatively high latitude and thus more fit for sightseers to have a bird's-eye-view of the grand landscape. The landscape will be the most magnificent when there is a sea of clouds or it snows or at sunset or sunrise.

Beside mountain peaks, Wulingyuan has more than 100 caves, and of them, the Yellow Dragon Cave in Suoxiyu Ravine is the best known. Composed of four floors, the cave has a lake, two rivers, three waterfalls, 13 halls and 96 corridors in the length of 15 kilometers. The largest hall can accommodate more than 10,000 people. Stalactites in different size, shape and color hang on the ceilings and stand on the ground in the cave. A piece of stalactite, which is only about 10 centimeters in diameter but 19.2 meters high, is the most fantastic. No one knows how many years it takes for the stalactite to take shape in the dripping of water.

Virgin forests cover 80 percent of the entire Wulingyuan area. There are more than 3,000 higher plant species, more than the total in a country or even a continent. Many of them are rare ancient plants and some are unique to China. For example, the ancient ginkgo trees are called "living fossils in the natural heritage." The valuable dove trees are in blossom in early Spring, when the flowers look like doves all over the trees, and they are thus called Chinese dove trees. The sparsely populated dense forests and high mountains certainly make a paradise for birds and animals. It is roughly estimated that there are some 110 species of birds there, and there are also such wild animals as tiger and leopards.

Wuliangyuan has been sparsely populated for a long time and its ecological system has remained intact. Experts say that disastrous weather, water and soil erosion, rockslides and pests have never happened here over the past thousands of years.

The area is rich in water. The winding brooks come from springs, forming ponds, flowing down as waterfalls from mountains and finally running into lakes. The streams never dry up even in serious drought. The place along the Golden Whip Stream in Zhangjiajie is one of the most beautiful scenic spots. The stream of five or six kilometers runs through forests and valleys, and tranquility reigns where the water runs.

Not as well known as Zhangjiajie, Suoxiyu Ravine has scenes as beautiful as those in Zhangjiajie. Mountains are grotesque, water crystal clean, cave quiet and bridge perilous here. Those bridges are works of nature. Some are 10 meters long and less than one meter wide across ravines more than 100 meters deep, and they look really perilous. A travelling route in the ravine is called "Five kilometer painting corridor." Once walking in the corridor, one will realize that the saying "walking in the valley is like travelling in a painting" is indeed true.

Although the traffic is inconvenient to Wulingyuan, the place is not totally cut off from the outside world. Villages scatter sporadically in the green mountains and blue waters. Bamboo leaves are fluttering in the wind and smoke is spiraling from kitchens, presenting a plain and simple pastoral landscape.

093 Precipitous peaks add magnificence to the Wulingyuan Scenic Area.

094 Most peaks in Wulingyuan Scenic Area look like pillars or awls chopped out with a knife or an ax.

094

095

095 The Gold Whip Stream, about six kilometers long, is the most beautiful spot in the scenic area.

096 A sea of peaks. More than 3,000 peaks are counted at Wulingyuan, mostly rising 200 meters from the ground.

096

097

097 The Peak of Imperial Writing Brushes on Mount Tianzi at Wulingyuan.

098 Inside the Yellow Dragon Cave. The Karst cave is 15 meters deep, enough to hold 10,000 people.

098

099 A "traditional Chinese painting" done with the ink-splashing technique. Nature is the "painter".

100 The "lobster flower" unique of the Wulingyuan area.

101 Photo shows a plant that belongs to a rare species of the Maglietia family. The Wulingyuan area is home to numerous rare plant species. It boasts most of the 13 species of gymnosperm identified so far across the world.

102 Locals call this bird the "water-carrying chicken" for the bit "bag" dangling from its neck, with which it stores water for consumption of three or four days.

103 Giant salamanders, a species under state protection, are one of the rare animals found in the area.

104 Peaks shrouded in clouds.

100

101

102

103

104

◀ 099

Huanglong Scenic and Historic Interest Area

Huanglong, or the "Yellow Dragon", is a scenic spot on the plateau in northwestern Sichuan Province, southwest China. It features snow-capped mountains as magnificent as those in Canada, primitive forests as beautiful as those in Colorado of the United States and a canyon as picturesque as that of Wyoming. Those travertine pools match those in the Yellow Stone National Park. A mountain separates Huanglong from the Jiuzhaigou, also a most famous scenic spot. To get to Huanglong from Jiuzhaigou, one has to travel well over 100 kilometers along a highway that winds up and down the mountain.

Huanglong covers an area of 700 square kilometers. It rises from 1,700 meters above sea level to 5,000 meters on an average. The peak, which stands 5,588 meters above sea level, is covered with snow all the year round.

Travertine formations form the most unique, most salient feature of this scenic spot.

Over the thousands upon thousands of years, water from melted snow and surface water have combined to form currents flowing beneath porous limes stones and, in the process, calcium carbonate substances in rocks were dissolved in those undercurrents. From time to time, such undercurrents emerged from underground. As these currents flowed, calcium carbonate carried in the water crystallized and stuck to rocks, grass and even feathers that happened to be on their way. Travertine formations were formed as a result, due to such factors as water temperature and declining of atmospheric pressure.

The rolling terrain at Huanglong helped form travertine of various shapes — travertine pools, travertine shoals and travertine waterfalls, for which the area has become known as a "natural travertine museum". Travertine landscapes are mostly found in Huanglong, Zhaduo and Er'daohai gullies 3,000-3,600 meters above sea level. What merits special mention is that travertine landscapes in these gullies are in different stages of evolution — those that are still in the making, those that are degenerating and those that have degenerated. That's why it doesn't take much time for visitors to learn the entire process of travertine evolution.

The Yellow Dragon Gully is where travertine landscapes are most concentrated. It is seven kilometers long and up to two kilometers wide. Travertine formations in the gully totaled 3,600 meters in length. Moreover, they are naturally arranged in such a way as to look like a Chinese dragon, hence the gully's name "yellow dragon".

About 3,400 travertine pools of various sizes and shapes are found at different heights in gully. The pools look like pearls strung up. There are eight groups of pools. Some pools are several hundred square meters large, and there are also pools as small as a straw hat. Some are round or in the shape of a fan, and still others resemble lotus seedpods or flowers. Beds and sides of the pools are creamy or light yellow in color, but the pools appear colorful due to the deposited substances on their beds and reflections of the surrounding mountains, trees and clouds. Scooping up water with your cupped hands, you will find water is crystal clean and refreshing. All this makes the gully a fairyland on the earth.

The largest group of colorful pools is called Five-Color Pools, which is situated 3,500 meters above sea level. In an area of 21,000 square meters, 683 colorful pools are counted.

105

Water in the pools is very shallow, gently brimming from one pool to another. Seen from afar, the pools look like jade plates. The word "colorful" is far from being good enough to describe the beauty of the gully. In winter, when the gully is covered with snow, and all is white — the trees, the mountains and the frozen water falls.

In the middle section of the Huanglong Gully, there is a 1,300-meter long travertine shoal, its narrowest section measuring 40 meters and the widest 122 meters. There is a kind of ridge-like slope, where it is difficult for calcium carbonate substances to settle and form pools. So, the water flows down, spreading all over the slope and, as a result, calcium carbonate came to stick to the surface of the slope and form a shoal covered by layers of calcium that look like fish scales. Golden color is predominant, studded by creamy white, gray and dark green. Getting atop the slope and overlooking the gully, one sees a golden outstretching ridge covered by calcium-carbonate scales and washed by spreading water. A huge "golden dragon", indeed. Experts say that this is the best preserved, the largest, the longest and the most colorful surface travertine shoal in the world.

The gully also has the world's longest collapse travertine structure — in fact a cliff on the second terrace of the gully. Travertine deposits falling down from the "golden dragon" abruptly collapse here and form a light yellow cliff, 10 meters high and 40 meters wide. The thick travertine layer on the cliff surface looks like a curtain or waterfall.

Travertine waterfalls are seen here and there in the gully. Once stepping into the gully, one, after passing the first colorful pool group, sees water flowing down from the shoulder of the stone wall that stands 10 meters high and is 60 meters long. The terraced terrain divides the waterfall into dozens of smaller falls, with some looking like pearls fall apart from a broken string. The cliff behind the waterfalls is covered by lung-shaped or plate-shaped travertine, with golden tone looming. All this combines to make the waterfall magnificent and beautiful.

The Zhaga Waterfall, which is located in the primitive forests in the Zhaga Gully, is 93 meters high and 35-40 meters wide. This waterfall has the longest drop of elevation in the country and is also the highest-situated travertine waterfall — 3,176-3,270 meters above sea level.

Plants grow sparsely amidst the colorful pools, waterfalls and shoals washed over by shallow flowing water. The plants are either above the water surface or submerged under water. The travertine pieces formed by calcium carbonate substance depositing on the trunks, boughs, stalks and leaves stand like weirdly looking rocks, or like willow trees, all suggestive of Chinese artificial rockery. The most representative of all is the Rockery Pool area, covering 20,000 square meters. There are 330 smaller pools grouped together, with some pools inside other pools and overgrown with bushes and flowers. This presents a dazzling array of artificial rockery of various sizes and shapes.

Primitive forests greet tourists when they first step into the gully. Walking along the stone or log-covered pathway, one has a feeling that one has entered the Jurassic Period. Everything is preserved in the way it looked millions of years ago. The string of colorful pools sit there quietly as if they have never been disturbed over the centuries.

As a matter of fact, travertine formations have ever been slowly growing. A stone pagoda and a stone house in the middle of two large travertine pools, for example, have been largely buried by the growing travertine, showing only the pagoda tip and the house roof in the limpid water. But they are not really old. According to archaeological studies, the pagoda and the house were built in the Ming Dynasty (1368-1644). So they are 600 years old or so at most.

Snow-capped peaks, glaciers, the plateau, the ethnic minority groups dwelling in the area, the primitive forests, the giant panda, the gold monkey and so on are all intoxicating. But what is most rare of all is the travertine landscape. It needs people's care because the travertine substance is extremely fragile. Once trampled carelessly, the beauty wrought by nature over the millions of years could be damaged once and for all.

The Huanglong or Yellow Dragon Scenery Area was listed as a site of World Natural Heritage in December 1992.

106

105 Pools at Huanglong have low banks and hence shallow water, flowing gently from the upper pools to lower ones.

106 There are 3,400 pools at different heights in the Huanglong scenic area.

107 The most majestic travertine waterfall is 14 meters high and 68 meters wide, washing down the terraced terrain.

摄影／王达军

109

110

108 This travertine shoal at Huanglong is 1,300 meters long. It is the longest, largest and best preserved of its kind in the world.

109 The snow-capped Xuebaoding Peak stands 5,588 meters above sea level and is revered by local ethnic Tibetans as a holy mountain.

110 Pools in the Huanglong scenic area are colorful, due to the deposited substances in the pools and the reflections of the surrounding mountains, trees, clouds and the blue sky.

◄ *108*

111 At the Huanglong scenic area, the first snow comes in mid-September and the last snow in early May of the following year.

112 Pools at Huanglong remain blue and limpid though the surroundings are covered with snow in Winter.

113 Rockery-like travertine formations.

114 The Zhaga Waterfall in Muni Gully is 93 meters high. It is the largest of its kind China in terms of head drop.

111

112

113

The Mountain Resort and Outlying Temples, Chengde

Chengde City, which lies some 200 kilometers to the north of Beijing, was once China's summer capital.

In the early 17th century, Chengde was only a small village with a few dozen households. In 1703, Emepror Kangxi of the Qing (1644-1911) Dynasty decided to build for himself a palace complex here. It took 89 years to complete the grand project. By 1792, the project, spanning the reigns of three emperors, namely, Kangxi, Yongzheng and Qianlong, was finished. Emperor Kangxi named it "Summer Resort."

The Summer Resort covers 5.64 square kilometers of land, twice the size of the Summer Palace in Beijing. This largest imperial garden in China encompasses three areas — the palace area, lake and plain area, and hilly area.

The palace area is in the southern part of the Summer Resort. Like the Forbidden City in Beijing, it is divided into the administrative area in the fore and living quarters in the rear. What is different is that the Forbidden City can't be more magnificent and splendid but buildings in the palace area of the Summer Resort look much simpler, smaller and less colorful. The black bricks and tiles are rather suggestive of the quadrangle walled courtyard in North China.

The main hall of the administrative area, Danbo Jingcheng Hall, or the Hall of Indifference to Oneself and Devotion to the State, occupies 600 square meters. It was built during the reign of Emperor Kangxi and was rebuilt under Emperor Qianlong. Nanmu, a precious timber from Southwest China, was the main building material. In rainy days, the fragrance of the timber permeates the hall. The main structure in the imperial residential area is called Yanbo Zhishuang Hall, or the Hall of Mist and Comfort. It is one of the 36 scenic spots that bear inscriptions of Emperor Kangxi.

Water surface makes up 10 percent of the total area of the Summer Resort, and this exemplifies a most salient feature of traditional Chinese garden design.

Dikes and islets divide the 29-hectare water surface into seven smaller "lakes", embodying a sort of refined artistic taste. Of the eight isles on the water surface, the most beautiful are the Yizhou, Huanbi and Yuese Jiangshen islets. Looking down from a higher place, one finds that the islets, in shape, resemble "ling zhi", a magic fungus with three stems. Ancient Chinese believed that ling zhi had miraculous curative powers and therefore symbolized good luck. The stems are in fact sections of the dike, which is modeled after the Su Tongpo Dike in the West Lake in Hangzhou City, Zhejiang Province. Su was a great poet and politician of the Song Dynasty. The dike named after him was built when he served as the city's magistrate.

Both Emperor Kangxi and Emperor Qianlong loved southern China's gardens. As luck had it, Chengde in northern China possessed all natural conditions for building southern-China-style gardens. The emperors ordered creation of scenes modeled after those in southern China they loved so much. In this Summer Resort, we find imitations of the Garden of Gentle Waves and the Garden of Lion Forest in Suzhou, Misty Rain Hall on Lake Nanhu in Jiaxing, and Golden Mountain Isle in Zhenjiang.

When construction was completed in the lake area, the lake came to be lined with beautiful willow trees, with water lapping up the bank and buildings half hidden in trees or reflected in the limpid water. The lakes were girdled by hills, and islets studded the water surface. Emperor Kangxi was so pleased that he said in one of his poems, "the natural scenery here is more beautiful than the West Lake."

To the north of the lake area is the plain area where feminine beauty in the lake area, which is characteristic of southern China, is replaced by the majestic beauty of the northern wilderness. The center of the plain area is Wanshu Garden, or Garden of Ten Thousand Trees, which was venue of im-

115

perial feasts.

In the northwest of the Summer Resort we find vast tracts of natural mountains, which make up four-fifths of the Summer Resort's area. Gurgling creeks wash through the thick forests which are the haven for wild animals. The area is permeated with primitiveness. Emperor Qianlong once remarked that the Summer Resort was a miniature of the country. Southern land crisscrossed by canals, northern grasslands and western mountains are all found here. And the buildings embody the quintessence of the architecture from across the country. All these combine to make the Summer Resort a place where best traditional Chinese architecture and garden design are displayed.

Why did the Qing emperors earmarked a large amount of cash to build such a large palace compound even though the newly founded Qing Dynasty was yet to be consolidated? Underlying the name of "Summer Resort" was a political farsightedness of appeasing the tribes in the north and consolidating the rule of the new dynasty over the country.

More directly, Emperor Kangxi would go hunting, leading thousands upon thousands of troops, each autumn starting 1682, in the Mulan hunting ground to the north of the Great Wall. Because the hunting usually lasted three to five months, establishment of a large temporary dwelling place became necessary. Hunting was in name. It amounted to a military exercise, a show of the dynasty's military might. The move aimed at honing military skills of the imperial troop, thus sending clear signals to the ethnic groups living beyond the Great Wall that it was wise to do nothing provocative.

In 1708, Emperor Kangxi came to stay in the Summer Resort for the first time. He was to come and stay for six months almost every year. Most emperors after him would, too, come and stay for some time every year, bringing with them court ministers and generals for the handling of state affairs. While enjoying themselves and handling state affairs, the emperors had another thing in mind - strengthening relations with China's ethnic minority groups.

In the 17th and 18th centuries, smallpox epidemic frequently occurred in China. Many ethnic Mongolian princes and nobles were therefore afraid of going to Beijing for imperial audience. In view of this, a court edict was issued to the effect that Mongolian noblemen and princes not immune to smallpox may have audience with the emperor in Chengde. As time went by, an unwritten rule came to be established, allowing nobles of ethnic minority groups to see the emperor who was staying in the Summer Resort to "escape from the summer heat in Beijing". The emperor would then busy himself giving honors, titles, gifts and feasts to the nobles. In July 1780, The sixth Panchen Lama, the second most important political and religious leader in Tibet, next only to the Dalai Lama, paid his respect to Emperor Qianlong in the Summer Resort. At a ceremony celebrating his 70th birthday, the emperor invited the Panchen Lama to sit abreast with him, on a chair at the side of the imperial throne, in front of those Mongolian princes, court officials and foreign envoys. This was the highest honor ever given by a Qing emperor to a leader of an ethnic minority group.

Twelve lamaseries were built in the east and north beyond the walls of the resort in order to accommodate the religious belief of the Mongolian and Tibetan ethnic groups. Two of them were built during the reign of Emperor Kangxi and ten during the reign of Emperor Qianlong. People habitually called these lamaseries the "eight outer temples".

These temples are magnificent with glazed tiles, including gilded tiles, in contrast with the imperial residences in the Summer Resort, which are mostly structure of black bricks and tiles.

Commoners were forbidden to enter some of these temples. Even for those officials who were allowed entry, there were stringent rules on what part of such a temple was open to officials of what specific rank. The sites and layouts of the temples were all decided by the emperors themselves. Many tablets and couplets bear inscriptions of the emperors. The inscriptions record the reasons why these temples were built. To name just a few: The Puning or Universal Peace Temple was built for the grand gathering attended by Emperor Qianlong and chieftains of four Mongolian nobles. The Xumi Fushou or Longevity and Happiness Temple was built to accommodate the Panchen Lama. The Anyuan or Eternal Stability Temple was intended to commemorate an imperial edict that permitted the Dashi Dawa Tribe, a branch of the ethnic Mongolian group, to settle down in Chengde. The Pule or Universal Happiness Temple was built in honor of some ethnic Kazakhs and Mongolian tribes who had submitted themselves to the authority of the central government. These temples testify to the unity of the various ethnic groups in China and the unification of the country.

The heyday of the Summer Resort and the eight outer temples began disappearing after Emperor Qianlong died. The emperor visited the resort 59 times in his lifetime. Emperors after him, however, increasingly estranged from the resort. On order of Empress Dowager, the de facto ruler of China in the late 19th century and early 20th, the government ceased to earmark any money for repairs and maintenance of the Summer Resort outright in 1898.

In 1994, the Summer Resort in Chengde and the surrounding temples entered the UNESCO list of World's Cultural Heritage.

115 A glimpse of the Chengde Summer Resort.

116 Putuo Zongchen Temple, the largest of the eight "outer temples", which is modeled after the Potala Palace in Lhasa. It was completed in 1771 in celebrating the 60th birthday of the Qing Emperor Qianlong.

116

118

117 Photo shows the Jinshan Islet, where main Taoist god used to be enshrined.

118 Photo shows Zhijinyun Dike, which is modeled on the Su Dongpo Dike on the West Lake in Hangzhou.

119 The Yanyu Pavilion is modeled after the building of the same name on the Nanhu Lake in Jiaxing, Zhejiang Province.

◄117

119

120

121

122

120 Magnificence of the eight outer temples poses a sharp contrast to a beauty of simplicity that characterizes the main palace halls in the Summer Resort.

121 The Pule Temple.

122 The Wenjin Hall, an imperial library.

123

124

123 The 1,000-hand and 1,000-eye Goddess of Mercy in the Dachenzhi Pavilion. Some 27 meters tall and weighing 110 tons, this is the largest wooden Buddhist figure in the world.

124 The Danbo Jingcheng Hall.

Temple and Cemetery of Confucius and the Kong Family Mansion in Qufu

In human history, probably no man is more respected than Confucius. For well over 2,000 years, the sage was worshipped by the Chinese of one generation after another.

Confucius was born in 551 BC, when China was torn apart by various dukedoms or states which fought one another incessantly. People were barely able to eke out a living, and society was morally degenerating. How to bring about a well organized, harmonious and happy society? This became a pressing issue. It was against this background that Confucius founded Confucianism, which calls for using ethical codes and rituals to guide people's behavior and make them love each other so as to restore order of society and family based on a hierarchical system. His followers later followed up his ideas. As a result, Confucianism eventually became the mainstream of the traditional Chinese culture.

Confucius began teaching in his 20s, and became reputed as an educator in about ten years. Before him, education was the privilege for children of the nobility. Confucius was the first to challenge the system by setting up a private school. The sage had 3,000 disciples all his life, including 72 who were recognized as prominent for their academic or political achievements. In feudal times, until China became a republic in the early 20th century, the *Analects* of Confucius and other Confucian classics were textbooks that all Chinese scholars were obliged to study.

At 51, Confucius was given an official post in the state of Lu, roughly in what is now Shandong Province, east China. But he resigned before long, saying that he did not want to mix up with those whose ideas and values he found impossible to share. So he started touring the different states, trying to persuade their rulers into accepting his political ideas. The attempt failed. Fourteen years of trekking around made him say, with stoic humor, that he was like a dog without a kennel. At 68, Confucius went back to his home town – Qufu - in the Lu State, where he taught his students and collected and collated classics until he died in 479 BC, at 73.

Although he did not get his due in his lifetime, Confucius was treated extremely generously after his death. All this treatment is reflected in the Confucius Temple, Confucius Family Mansion and Confucius Woods in Qufu.

The year after his death, his home was converted into a temple, displaying his clothes, hats, harps, carts and books. Worshipping ceremonies were held there regularly. In every provincial capital, prefecture capital and county seat, Confucius temples were erected. In Korea, Japan, Vietnam, Indonesia and Singapore today, places for worshipping Confucius can also be found. The oldest and the largest of all the Confucius temples in the world is of course the one in Qufu - Confucius' home town.

At first, worshipping Confucius was a family matter for Confucius' posterity. Liu Bang, the founder and the first emperor of the Han Dynasty (206 BC-220 AD), paid his homage to Confucius during an inspection tour that took him to Qufu. By doing so, he set an example to be followed by all dynasties.

Sixty years later, Emperor Wudi of the Han Dynasty proscribed all non-Confucian schools of thought and espoused Confucianism as the orthodox state ideology. Confucianism became the mainstay of the traditional Chinese culture from then on. In history, 11 emperors personally went to Qufu to worship Confucius.

The Confucius Temple underwent expansion and revamping time and again and in the Ming Dynasty (1368-1644), it took on the look and size as we see today. In 1511, a rebel peasant army entered the temple. Confucius' posterity fled and the architecture was damaged. In view of this, the emperor then ordered that the Qufu County seat a few kilometers away be moved to the side where the Confucius

125

Temple sat.

In layout, the Confucius Temple is modeled on the imperial palace in Beijing. It is 600 meters long from north to south and 140 meters wide from east to west. There are nine courtyards sitting astride the north-south axis line. The first three courtyards serve chiefly as a part leading up to the main ones. So the sizes are rather small. A passage way is lined with ancient cypress and pine trees. A feeling of respect naturally wells up in a visitor when he or she enters the temple. The following courtyards contain libraries and the Imperial Tablet Pavilion that shelters the tablets inscribed with the titles and honors conferred on Confucius by emperors and also tablets recording the construction of the temple. There is also the Hall of the Sage's Deeds, where stone carvings display Confucius' activities in his life time.

The Dacheng Hall, or the Hall of the Greatest of All Sage, is the main building of the temple. It is the highest building in the temple, with red walls and golden glazed tiles. In the center of the hall is the shrine of Confucius. The colored sculpture of Confucius is flanked by his disciples. A two-meter high open-air platform in front of the hall is where ceremonies for worshipping Confucius were staged. In the east and west wings are two rows of houses where the memorial tablets for 156 outstanding Confucian scholars in various dynasties are placed.

In the east of the Confucius Temple is the Confucius Mansion which, consisting of a few dozen courtyards, is the dwelling place for Confucius' posterity.

In 195 BC, the first title of lord was conferred on Confucius' posterity, which marked the beginning of honors and titles lavishly showered on Confucius' posterity. In 1055, Confucius' 46th- generation great grandson was made the "Duke of Yan". This hereditary title for the eldest male among the sages' lineal descendants was to be handed down generation after generation until 1935 when the sage's 77th-generation great grandson got the title.

The Duke of Yan had responsibility for worshipping Confucius and seeing to it that the Confucius clan would become ever prosperous in terms of population. He also had a say in the affairs of Qufu County. The magistrate of Qufu must be a member of the Confucius clan and should be recommended by the duke. Not another Chinese family has enjoyed such special treatment as the Confucius clan over the last millennia.

According to the clan's rule, Confucius' posterity down the direct line of decent should live in the Confucius Mansion in order to serve and worship the master. There are also nine courtyards on an axis line in the mansion. The mansion combines the administrative areas, living quarters and gardens. There are 463 rooms in all. The buildings in the fore are for clan members to handle administrative affairs and meet visitors. The courtyards in the rear are living quarters. The two parts are partitioned by a gate. A huge amount of historical records, relics, ancient costumes and utensils are stored in the mansion.

The Confucius Woods is actually the graveyard of Confucius and his posterity. It is located one kilometer to the north of Qufu. A "divine avenue" leads from the Confucius Woods to the town gate of Qufu. According to the clan's rule, clan members in the following categories cannot be buried here after their death: Those who die not yet 18 years old; those sentenced to death; those female members who are married out; and those who have become Buddhist monks. In the two-square-kilometer graveyard 100, 000 clan members are buried. This is the largest and most lasting clan graveyard in the world. The area is bristling with towering trees.

Confucius' tomb is in the center of the woods. Its red

wall measures half a kilometer. On the right side of the Confucius' tomb the sage's son is buried and in the front, his grandson. This kind of burial style is called "taking the son by hand and carrying the grandson in bosom".

Not far away from the tomb are three small rooms, where Confucius' disciple Zi Gong lived, guarding his master's tomb. According to historical records, Zi Gong guarded Confucius' tomb for six years after the sage's death, while other disciples, only three years. He did this entirely out of his respect for his teacher, taking into account that Confucius at that time did not enjoy much honor as he did later.

Apart from Confucius' tomb, the most majestic is Lady Yu's tomb. She was daughter of Emperor Qianlong of the Qing Dynasty (1644-1911). In the Qing dynasty, marriage between the ruling Manchus and the Han ethnic people was banned. So the emperor first made her an adopted daughter of a Han court official, whose surname was Yu, and then married her to a 72nd-generation great grandson of Confucius, who was Duke of Yan at the time.

A tomb in the Confucius Woods is worth special mention. It belongs to Kong Shangren, who was a 64th-generation great grandson of Confucius and also author of the famous play *Peach Flower Fan*.

The Confucius Temple, Confucius Woods and Confucius Mansion are symbols of ancient Chinese worshipping of Confucianism. The 100,000 or so relic pieces are important physical materials for studying Chinese history, culture and arts. In December 1994, the Confucius Temple, Confucius Mansion and Confucius Woods came to be inscribed on the UNESCO list of World Cultural Heritage.

126

125 Confucius (551BC-479BC), founder of Confucianism, which was China's dominating ideology for well over 2,000 years before the country became a republic in 1911. The portrait was done by an anonymous painter of the Ming (1368-1644) Dynasty.

127

128

126 The Confucius Temple.

127 Inside one of the 463 chambers in the Confucius Mansion.

128 The garden in the Confucius Mansion. It underwent revamping three times with donations from Chinese monarchs and court officials who had blood relations with the Confucian clan.

129

130

129 The Dacheng Hall, or the Hall of the Greatest Sage. It is the main building in the Confucius Temple, where official ceremonies were held for worshipping Confucius.

130 A total of 55 stone tablets are counted in 13 imperial pavilions in the Confucius Temple. These are inscribed with words about tributes paid by monarchs and court officials to the Chinese sage.

131 A sculpture of the Chinese sage is enshrined in the Hall of the Greatest Sage. Hung above the sculpture are tablet inscribed with eulogies written by some emperors in honor of Confucius.

131 

132

133

134

132 The Apricot Terrace.

133 The tomb of Confucius in the center of the Confucius Woods.

134 Photo shows other tombs in the Confucius Woods, a two square kilometer area where 100,000 members of the Confucian clan are buried.

135 Flanking the pathway leading to the tomb of Confucius tomb are animal and human figures of stone, forming a squad of guard for the sage in the nether world.

135

The Potala Palace at Lhasa

Tibet is mysterious and a faraway place in many people's mind's eye. An atmosphere of religion shrouds the snow-covered plateau inhabited mostly by ethnic Tibetans. The atmosphere is so strong that it seems as if time and man were frozen by it.

The Potala Palace is in Lhasa, capital of China's Tibet Autonomous Region. In the Tibetan language, the word "potala" means the "dwelling place" of Avilokiteshvara, the Buddhist Goddess of Mercy. It is where the Dalai Lamas of all generations held their political and religious activities and where they stayed when alive and after they die as well.

The Potala Palace was not built originally as a holy place for Buddhism. Songtsen Gampo (619-650) brought all the tribes on the Qinghai-Tibet plateau under his control in seventh century AD and established the Tubo Kingdom of his own. In 641, upon marrying Princess Wencheng of the Tang Dynasty, Songtsen Gampo decided to build a grand palace to accommodate her and to serve as a memorial to this important event. Unfortunately, the original palace was destroyed by lightning and war damage in the ninth century, when the Tubo kingdom was split.

In the year 1645, the central government officially appointed the Fifth Dalai Lama as the political and religious chief of the Tibetan local government. He then started to reconstruct the Patala Palace. The Potrang Karpo, or White Palace, was completed three years later. Construction of the Potrang Marpo, or Red Palace, was started in 1690 to remember the Fifth Dalai Lama and accommodate the stupa where his remains were kept for worshipping. The project was completed four years later. Some renovations in the later period extended the palace to its present size.

The Potala Palace is perched upon Marpo Ri hill - in fact occupying almost the entire hill. Looked from afar, the color of red alternates with that of white on the wall of the palace while the golden roof is grand and splendid. The palace looks like a Tibetan castle with stone and wood exterior structures, while the roof assumes the style of a typical Han palace. Both the exterior and interior decorations are in the style similar to that of Nepalese palaces and temples.

The structure of the Potala Palace is beyond the imaginations of many. It is 115 meters in height. It looks as if it has 13 stories, but in fact it has just nine. The wall is eight meters thick and becomes gradually thinner up to its top, where the wall is still one meter thick. Molten iron was injected into some part of the walls, which are therefore really invulnerable. Looking down from atop the palace, you can see a city crowded with low Buddhist dwellings, civilian houses and workshops. There is striking contrast between different parts in its inner structure: the halls are quite spacious while the windows are extremely narrow; and the walls are quite thick while the corridors are very narrow. All these seem to manifest the mighty power of the Buddhist doctrine and the solemnity of the Buddhist world.

The Potala Palace is composed of two parts. The Red Palace is in the center, and the White Palace fans to the east and west. The entire palace has more than 2,000 rooms. The White Palace has seven stories and is where the Dalai Lamas of all generations lived and exercised their political power. The largest room is the Eastern Hall on the fourth floor, and it was here that the Dalai Lamas were enthroned and from here he ruled Tibet. The Chamber of Sunshine on the top floor is divided into the Eastern Chamber of Sunshine and the Western Chamber of Sunshine, and it can let in sunshine all day long. This is where the Dalai Lama stayed in winter. The Chamber of Sunshine has guestrooms, rest rooms and rooms where the Dalai Lamas practice Buddhist

136

scriptures. The old rules stipulated that only Buddhist monks above the fourth rank could enter the Western Chamber of Sunshine.

The Red Palace, which is composed several halls, is the highest complex in the Potala Palace, where the holy stupas of successive Dalai Lamas are worshipped. Among the eight holy stupas, the one that holds the remains of the Fifth Dalai Lama, which is in the center, is the largest and most splendid. It is 14.85 meters in height and the whole tower is decorated with gold weighing 110,000 ounces in total, plus more than 10,000 diamonds, pearls and jade pieces embedded on it. The other stupas are also decorated with gold, diamonds, pearls and jade pieces. Therefore, they are extremely valuable.

The portrait of Emperor Qianlong of the Qing Dynasty (1644-1911) and his memorial tablet are placed in the highest hall of the Red Palace for people to pay tribute to. Written in Chinese, Manchu, Tibetan and Mongolian languages on the tablet are the words "Long live our emperor". Starting the Seventh Dalai Lama, Dalai Lamas of all generations would come here on January 1 by the Tibetan calendar to pay tribute to the portrait and memorial tablet.

The Potala Palace is a world of murals, tankas (traditional Tibetan paintings), Buddha statues and other cultural relics. Colorful murals can be seen in almost all the halls in the palace. Their contents involve the origin of the Tibetan ethnic group, the history of every sect in the Tibetan school of Buddhism, Buddhist stories, profiles and stories about the Dalai Lamas, as well as important historical events. For example, such events as the Dalai Lama going to Beijing to pay tribute to the emperor and Princess Wencheng married to Songtsen Gampo are depicted on the murals.

At the back of the hill is the back garden of the Potala Palace, which is known as the Pond of Dragon King. In the middle of the garden there is a lake, on which there are small islands. At the foot of the hill is a scenic spot called "snow", where the printing house to print Buddhist scriptures and other workshops are located. Around the foot of the hill are walls and blockhouses guarding the palace.

The Potala Palace was inscribed on the list of World Cultural Heritage in 1994. As extended items, Jokhang Temple and Norbulingka were inscribed on the list in November 2000 and December 2001, respectively.

Located in the center of Lhasa, Jokhang Temple is the holiest shrine for the Tibetan school of Buddhism. It is also the largest, able to accommodate tens of thousands of lamas to conduct religious ceremonies. The temple was built in 647 AD after Songtsen Gampo married Nepalese Princess Tritsun and Princess Wenchang from the Tang Dynasty. Both princesses had brought Buddhist scriptures and Buddha statues, and the temple was built just to accommodate these scriptures and statues for people to pay tribute to. The temple was not as big as it is now at the time and it had only eight halls. Several renovations have expanded the temple to its present size.

Jokhang Temple has a construction space of 25,000 square meters and more than 20 halls. The main hall in the center has four stories, and accommodates a gold-plated statue of Sakyamuni, founder of Buddhism, which was brought to Tibet by Princess Wencheng. Four statues of strongmen stand on the two sides, which are "dressed" the same way as Han Chinese of the Tang Dynasty. The statues were made to remember those who transported the statue of Sakyamuni from the Chinese capital to Tibet, according to historical records. Murals are painted on the four walls, including those depicting Princess Wenchang's arrival in Tibet and those about the construction of the temple.

In front of the temple is a three-meter high monument to commemorate the friendship between Tibet and the Tang Dynasty. Erected in 823 AD, the monument has inscriptions describing how the princess of the Tang Dynasty was married to the King of Tubo to cement the friendship.

Norbulingka, which means "Jeweled Garden" in Tibetan, lies in suburban Lhasa, about three kilometers to the west of the city center. Built in 1755, Norbulingka occupies an area of 360,000 square meters and is divided into three parts: the front park in the east, the central part of palaces and the part of forest in the west.

Starting from the 17th century, the Dalai Lama of consecutive generations would handle their political affairs and hold rituals and ceremonies in the park. They would spend summer here. The Dalai Lamas would come here in March every year and would not return to the Potala Palace until the end of October. Therefore, Norbulingka is also called "the summer palace" while the Potala Palace, "the winter palace." The boy chosen as the incarnation of a dead Dalai Lama was obliged to stay here to study Buddhist scriptures until he was old enough to be enthroned as the Dalai Lama of the next generation.

The UNESCO World Heritage Committee commented in its report: The Jokhang Temple and Potala Palace remain to the present day one of the most typical areas of the country in terms of their ancient buildings and their role as the political, economic, cultural, and religious center of Tibet. The Jokhang Temple is an exceptional Buddhist religious complex. Norbulingka is a masterpiece of Tibetan art. The beauty and originality of the architecture of these three sites, their ornamentation and harmonious integration in a striking landscape, add to their historic and religious interest.

137

138

136 The Buddhist wheel of law and the auspicious deer atop the main hall of Jokhang Temple.

137 A full view of the Potala Palace.

138 Photo shows the top of the Red Palace, where seven sets of "gold pinnacles" are counted.

139 Norbulingka, the "Jeweled Garden", was the summer palace of the Dalai Lama.

140 Potala Palace in early morning.

141 An aerial view of Jokhang Temple.

139

140

141

143

144

145

146

142 One of the 300 Buddha statues enshrined in Jokhang Temple.

143 A portrait of Songtsen Gampo (619-650), who brought all the tribes on the Qinghai-Tibet plateau under his control and established the Tubo Kingdom of his own. The portrait is worshipped in Potala Palace.

144 Potala Palace is a world of Buddhist sculptures, murals and other cultural relics. Photo shows the interior of a hall there.

145 This mural depicts the Dalai Lama of the 13th generation (1876-1933) paying tribute to Empress Dowager Cixi and Emperor Guangxu in Beijing. The mural is found in the hall that houses the stupa where the Dalai Lama's remains are kept for worshipping.

146 A sculpture of Princess Wencheng of the Tang Dynasty, who married King Songtsen Gampo in the year 641.

◀142

Ancient Building Complex in the Wudang Mountains

In the year 1412, ground was broken for reconstruction on Mount Wudang, a most famous scenic spot and a holy shrine of Taoism, more than 1,000 kilometers to the southwest of Beijing.

In 1994, 582 years later, these buildings were collectively inscribed on the UNESCO list of World Cultural Heritage. A report by the UNESCO World Heritage Committee describes them as a "perfect combination of typical Taoist architecture with natural landscape."

Taoism was founded 1,800 years ago in China. It is the only indigenous religion practiced in the country, relative to Buddhism, Christianity and Islam that are alien religions. Followers of Taoism have the lifelong pursuit of becoming immortal through self-cultivation, believing that the divine world embraces not only the heaven but also the earth. In their mind's eye, places with a surpassing scenic beauty are "lands of happiness" with channels leading to paradise - or "Heaven" as the Chinese choose to call it.

Mount Wudang, which occupies an area of 312 square kilometers in Central China' s Hubei Province, is exactly such a place. Far back in the 2nd century, it was already somewhat "holy", as host to those who came to practice austerities or just to live in seclusion, free from wars and social turmoil.

Mount Wudang already had a range of Taoist palaces, temples and monasteries in the Yuan Dynasty (1279-1368). Unfortunately, most of these were reduced to ruins in wars before the dynasty collapsed. It was Zhu Di, or Emperor Yongle of the Ming Dynasty (1368-1644), who ordered reconstruction and expansion of Taoist buildings on the mountain. During his reign, nine Taoist palaces (gong), nine large temples (guan) and 36 nunneries were built, along with 72 smaller temples and some pavilions. With the highest peak as the center, these are now found on the 72 surrounding peaks and on banks of 24 streams. Somewhere between 200, 000 and 300,000 soldiers and civilians spent 12 years building these structures, and the project exhausted the government coffers of nine southern China provinces.

At the time, the influence of Taoism was beginning to dwindle and moreover, Emperor of Yongle did not really believe in Taoism. Then why is it that the emperor spent so much money on Mount Wudang?

The emperor's inscriptions carved on some stone tablets seem to provide an answer. He did so, according to these inscriptions, to repay gods for their help in running the country, show filial piety to his parents and pray for the happiness of his people.

Zhu Di had been a prince before he usurped the imperial throne from Emperor Jianwen, his nephew, to become the third emperor of the Ming Dynasty. He had to justify what he had done. It so happened that his father Zhu Yuanzhang, the first emperor of the Ming Dynasty, believed in the Taoist God of Genuine Prowess, and that Mount Wudang was said to be the holy shrine of the god. By launching this project, Zhu Di tried to tell the entire country that he had the same faith as his father and therefore was a filial son, and that he and his father both had the protection of the same God of Genuine Prowess in their fight for power. In short, he wanted to make his people believe that his throne was divine-given.

Combination of the monarchical authority with the divine powers of the God of Genuine Prowess features the layout of those palaces and temples built under Emperor Yongle. These are divided into two parts: buildings on the mountains and those at its foot.

147

The Jingle Palace, literally the Palace of Purity and Happiness, lies at the foot of Mount Wudang. The temple, the first to be built under the reign of Emperor Yongle, is dedicated to the God of Genuine Prowess, who had been a prince of the legendary Jingle Kingdom before he became a Taoist god through 42 years' practice of austerities. According to a travelogue of the Ming Dynasty, the temple covered half of the area occupied by the city down the mountains and resembled the imperial palace. A road paved with flagstone connects the palace with the highest mountain peak 60 kilometers away.

The Xuanyue Gate, or the Gate of Divine Mystique, is the entrance of the mountainous scenic spot, the entrance of this "divine world", which is a land of lush green and tranquility covered with dense forests. Along the "Divine Road" up the mountain, there is a temple every 2.5 kilometers and a palace every 5 kilometers, and all have stories attributed to them. One is said to be where the God of Genuine Prowess practiced austerities and became immortal.

Divine power, no matter how great, must be submitted to monarchical authority. This unshakable principle of feudalism was strictly followed in construction of the Taoist buildings on Mount Wudang.

The Zixiao or Purple Skies Palace had been center of the Taoist structures on Mount Wudang before the Ming Dynasty, people of the previous dynasty, the Yuan, believing that the neighboring Nanyan or South Rock Palace was where the God of Genuine Prowess lived. Emperor of Yongle, however, designated Tianzhu or Heavenly Pillar Peak, the highest peak, as the center of this Taoist shrine. The peak overlooks all other peaks, and Emperor Yongle likened the peak to himself, with his court ministers paying tribute to him. On order of the emperor, a copper palace was built on the very top of the peak, which is 160 square meters in area. The structure is called the "Golden Palace" because it is a gold-plated structure and is modeled on an imperial building. A statute of the God of Genuine Prowess is worshipped in the Golden Palace. It is said that the statue, 1.86 meters high, was modeled on Emperor Yongle.

Three years after the Golden Palace was built, also on imperial order, a wall of rectangular stone slabs was constructed round it, and the palace was renamed "Purple Golden City". You've got to remember that Emperor of Yongle lived in the Forbidden City in Beijing, which is also known as the "Purple Forbidden City".

Down the mountain from this "Purple Golden City" is the Taihe Palace, alias Temple of Tao. In the Ming Dynasty, the Purple Golden City was forbidden, and the Temple of Tao was the last Taoist shrine they were allowed to enter.

The God of Genuine Prowess is not the highest Taoist god. Despite that, Emperor Yongle made his shrine the most imposing and magnificent of all Taoist shrines in the country. He personally took charge of the project, on which he issued more than 60 orders, and saw to it that everything would be done to his satisfaction. For a time, there were 4,000 Taoist monks and nuns on the mountain, who were chosen from among Taoists all over the country. In 1416, 3,100 people in 500 families elsewhere in China were moved to Mount Wudang, and were charged with producing food for those Taoist monks and nuns. Not long afterwards, 500 troops were dispatched to this imperial holy site. Ironically, Emperor Yongle had never been to the mountain before he died. Neither had any of the 15 Ming emperors after him.

Taoism stands for harmony between Man and nature,

believing that Man is an integral part of nature. This principle was strictly observed in construction of this Taoist shrine. On order of Emperor Yongle, felling of trees on the mountain was forbidden, and so was anything that may adversely affect the original landscape of the mountains.

The basic layout of the Taoist shrine has never changed although some more temples were constructed and some renovations were done after Emperor Yongle died. In 1552, Emperor Jiajing ordered renovation of 955 rooms and chambers in temples and palaces on the mountain. In 1642, peasant rebel troops under Li Zicheng burned down the local government office charged with administering religious affairs. With the collapse of the Ming Dynasty two years afterwards, the imperial Taoist shrine became open to the general public. No new buildings have been constructed ever since. Many temples and palaces have been deserted, despite repeated renovations.More than 200 buildings have been preserved to this day, which together have a construction space of 50,000 square meters. As always, these are home to Taoist monks and nuns. You need to spend five days visiting all these buildings.

148

149

147 Photo shows the copper statue of Xuanwu, which had been regarded as the guardian god of the north before it came to be worshipped as a Taoist god. Ancient Chinese pictured the god as a snake with the head of a turtle.

148 The Tainzhu Peak overlooks all other peaks in the scenic area.

149 Photo shows the Nanyan Palace, one of the numerous Taoist shrines "hanging" on cliffs.

150 Photo shows the Xuanyue Gate, entrance of Mount Wudang, which is seen as the line demarcation between the mortal and immortal worlds.

150

152

153

151 The Taihe Palace on Mount Wudang.

152 Photo shows the copper statue of the Taoist God of Genuine Prowess enshrined in the Golden Palace atop Mount Wudang.

153 Photo shows the copper palace on the top of Tianzhu Peak. The gilded palace is also known as the "Golden Palace".

154 The Taoist God of Genuine Prowess was once depicted as a snake with the head of a turtle. A bird's-eye-view of Mount Wudang's main peak coincides with this depiction.

154

◀151

156

157

155 A glimpse of the Taihe Palace on the top of Tianzhu Peak.

156 Photo shows the main hall of the Zixiao or Purple Skies Palace, the largest and best preserved Taoist temples on Mount Wudang.

157 Ridges of the Goden Palace are decorated with figurines of immortals and legendary animals.

◄ *155*

Lushan National Park

Of all the Chinese sites inscribed on the list of World Heritage, Mount Lushan has a somewhat special status, that of World Cultural Landscape.

Located in the north of Jiangxi Province and on the southern bank of the middle reaches of the Yangtze River, the scenic spot has a total area of 302 square kilometers. Several cities not quite far from the mountain are so hot in summer that they are called "ovens". Mount Lushan, however, is a cool oasis.

To know Mount Lushan, one must know something about its cultural background. When visiting it 1928, Chinese scholar Hu Shi (1891-1962) wrote in his travelogue, *A Trip to Lushan*, that three historical sites in the mountain represent three tendencies. The first is the Eastern Woods Temple, which represents the general trend for Buddhism, an alien religion, to assume distinct Chinese characteristics. The White Deer Cave, actually an ancient academy of learning, represents the trend for the Song School of Confucianism, or neo-Confucianism, to dominate Chinese thought for some 700 years after the 10th century. The third is the Guling Ridge that symbolizes the invasion of China by Western culture.

Eastern Woods Temple lies at the northwestern foot of Mount Lushan. In the year 381 AD, the eminent monk Huiyuan was passing by Mount Lushan and put up on the mountain for a couple of days at the invitation of a fellow Buddhist. His chance changed the history of the mountain. Historical records say that Huiyuan made up his mind to stay and give up his plan to go to the south since he found Mount Lushan was a peaceful place and good for cultivation of one's inner world. The local magistrate had a temple built for him in the year 386. This new temple was to the east of Western Woods Temple for his friend who had invited him to come. It was thus named the Eastern Woods Temple.

By Huiyuan's time, It had been some 300 years since Buddhism was brought into China. Even though, Buddhist scriptures were translated and lectured upon only in a rote way. Thus Buddhism was limited only to the intellectual circle and the upper class. Mysterious Learning, a metaphysical sect that had something to do with Buddhism, was quite popular at the time. It so happened that the Monk Huiyuan had a good ground in Buddhist philosophy, Mysterious Learning and Confucianism. When giving lectures on Buddhism, he integrated ideas of Confucianism and Mysterious Learning with those of Buddhism. As a result, those who had been confused about Buddhism came to understand it. More and more people came to the temple, and gradually the ideas of Buddhism began spreading across the country, and so did the reputation of the monk, Huiyuan.

In his 36 years on Mount Lushan, beside translating Buddhist scriptures, writing books on them and giving lectures, Huiyuan, with his knowledge, wisdom and broadmindedness, gathered a group of eminent monks and scholars around him. They set up the Pure Land Sect of Buddhism. According to this doctrine, as long as one recites the name of the Buddha, always keeps the "Western Paradise" in mind and gets rid of all human desires, one would be reborn in the Western Paradise after death. Since this Buddhist discipline is simple to practice, the Pure Land Sect became increasingly influential. Beginning with Huiyuan, Mount Lushan has been a most important Buddhist shrine in south China.

Mount Lushan is also a holy shrine of Taoism, China's indigenous religion.

A Taoist monk named Lu Jingxiu had visited many famous mountains before he arrived in Mount Lushan in the year 461 and decided to stay. Then he had a Taoist temple

158

built in the mountain. Those waterfalls, pine trees and bamboo groves made a very beautiful and peaceful environment for Taoist monks to practice their religion. Lu stayed on Mount Lushan for seven years. While there, he wrote about Taoism, transformed the organization of the Taoist hierarchy and established the Southern Sky sect of Taoism. Lu Jingxiu was canonized as Master Jianji (meaning "master of simplicity and tranquility"). The temple where he stayed has thus been called Jianji Temple.

In the year 405, a man who did not want to cater to vulgar taste of secular world came to the foot of the mountain. He said in one of his best-known poems that a bird in the cage always misses the forest it used to stay in. He gave up his official post for a life of drinking wine, writing poems and doing farming in the fields. He died of illness and poverty, but never regretted his choice. This person was Tao Yuanming, a most prominent poet in ancient China. The moral integrity of this poet has been admired by intellectuals of later generations. Tao Yuanming was born here in Lushan. After he died, many scholars came from other places to live in seclusion like him.

Mount Lushan is a place of tranquility and also a place for introspection.

In the valley of Wulaofeng Peak there stands the White Deer Cave Academy of Learning, one of the oldest and also one of the most influential institutions of learning in ancient China. It was Zhu Xi, one of the greatest scholars of Confucianism in the Song Dynasty (960-1279), to whom the regulation of the academy must be attributed.

Zhu Xi epitomized the Confucian school of idealist philosophy of the Song Dynasty and brought Confucianism to a new high. Until 1905, his interpretations of the classic works of Confucianism were compulsory textbooks for scholars intending to take part in imperial examinations for official posts. Zhu Xi was engaged in teaching for more than 50 years, when academies of learning were thriving. When he arrived in Lushan in 1179 to serve as an official, the White Deer Cave Academy of Learning had already become dilapidated. He had the academy rebuilt, bought fields for the scholars to do farming in their spare time, compiled textbooks and curriculums, set up rules for students and invited well known scholars to teach. He also collected a lot of classic books for the library. As a result, scholars came from all over the country and the academy became reputed as the best in the country. The goals, requirements, contents and method of the course of study established by Zhu Xi at the academy were to be followed by scholars of the later generations. The academy had witnessed ups and downs in the centuries until the mid-19th century when it was deserted.

Mount Lushan had witnessed its heyday from the fourth century to the 13th. There were as many as 500 Buddhist and Taoist temples on the mountain, and even in its less prosperous period, there were still as many as 300 temples. Different from other famous mountains, Lushan had a heavy ambience of culture and scholarship. It is Zhu Xi and his academy that made Lushan the mountain for Chinese intellectuals.

Chinese scholars or literati often wrote about mountains and rivers to vent their feelings, and many made friends with monks when they suffered frustrations in their political career. Mount Lushan was their favorite sanctuary. The Tang Dynasty poet Li Bai developed a liking for Taoism. Another Tang Dynasty poet, Bai Juyi, admired the noble characters of Poet Tao Yuanming. Both poets once had plans to build thatched houses to stay on Mount Lushan, and so did Zhu Xi, who was quite practical.

Chinese poets have written a lot of poems about various mountains. Of all these poems, only those about Mount Lushan have become household poems. Song Dynasty poet Su Shi wrote a poem on the wall of West Woods Temple, which goes:

Viewed horizontally, it's a ridge; vertically, a peak
And quite a different height from far or near
I can't recognize its true face because
I myself am on the mountain.

After making a trip to Big Woods Temple (Dalin), the Tang poet Bai Juyi wrote:

By the fourth month in the world
The flowers have already faded.
But the mountain temple peach buds
Have just gotten glorious.
I've deplore the loss of Spring
Couldn't find it anywhere,
Ignorant I moved right here.

Nowadays, the East Woods Temple and the Academy of White Deer Cave are still there; however, only the ruins of Jianji Temple remain. But there are many villas around Guling Ridge. Starting from the end of the 19th century, foreign missionaries began to lease land to construct villas there. It is estimated there are more than 600 villas in the styles of 18 countries. Catholic churches, Christian churches, Eastern Orthodox Church chapels and Islamic mosques mingle with the villas.

The UNESCO World Heritage Committee commented in 1996: Buddhist and Taoist temples, along with the Academy of White Deer Cave representing Confucian school of idealist philosophy, are blend effortlessly into a striking beautiful landscape. The landscape is of high aesthetic worth and well integrated with the spirit of the Chinese nation and its cultural life.

158 Pine trees on a precipitous cliff of Mount Lushan.

159 Hanpokou, the best place to enjoy the magnificent sight of Mount Lushan shrouded in clouds.

160

161

160 Lake Lulin at the foot of Mount Lushan.

161 Mount Lushan was once a center of Buddhism, Taoism and Confucianism.

162 The Brocade Valley on Mount Lushan.

162

163

164

163 Photo shows Huajing, ruins of Big Woods Temple, one of the three most famous Buddhist Temples on Mount Lushan. The temple inspired Tang Dynasty poet Bai Juyi to write one of his masterpieces.

164 A Western-style villa on Mount Lushan, a best-known summer resort in China.

165

166

167

168

169

165 A religious ceremony in progress in Eastern Wood Temple on Mount Lushan.

166 Photo shows the Eastern Wood Temple which, built in the year 386, was to become the birthplace of the Pure Land Sect of Buddhism.

167 The White Deer Cave, actually an ancient academy of learning, represents the trend for neo-Confucianism to dominate Chinese thought for some 700 years after the 10th century.

168 Mount Lushan is shrouded in clouds on an average of 200 days in a year, inspiring Song Dynasty poet Su Dongpo to write this famous line: "I cannot recognize its true face, because I myself am in the mountain".

169 A waterfall on Mountain Lushan.

Mount Emei and Leshan Giant Buddha

On the edge of Sichuan Basin in Southwest China, a mountain stretches some 200 kilometers and that is Mount Emei, one of the four most holy mountains of Buddhism.

An ocean was here 800 million years ago. In an orogenic or mountain-building movement, burning magma burst out of the ocean floor and turned into hard granite after becoming cold, finally creating a small continent. This is the original place of Mount Emei. The continent fell into the ocean twice and came out twice as well in the following 550 million years. Fossils of ancient extinct marine life in the mountain have been found as evidence to these changes.

A bird's-eye-view reveals that Mount Emei rises straight from the ground. Its highest peak, Wanfoding, or the Peak of Ten Thousand Buddhas, stands majestically 3,099 meters above sea level, with a relative altitude of 2,600 meters. Its top, the Golden Summit, overhangs on a precipitous cliff. Standing on the summit, one will feel proud that he or she is even higher than the mountain itself. When looking into the distance, however, one will see range after range of peaks and the sea of clouds, and all of a sudden, one will realize that man is so small compared with the grand mountain.

It is more than 60 kilometers from the mountain foot to the Golden Summit. Climbing up the mountain, one will experience four seasons. The climate is the same as its surrounding area at the mountain foot and belongs to subtropical one. It is neither warm nor cold in the waist of the mountain and its climate belongs to temperature zone. It becomes a bit cold a little higher up the mountain waist, which belongs to the sub-frigid zone climate. Finally one will experience the weather of Frigid Zone climate on the mountain peak. Because of the high altitude and low pressure, it is vary hard to cook food on the Golden Summit, where there are very few plants and animals. Only fir, bamboo and moss grow there. The branches and leaves of firs are drooping, indicating that they are often under the weight of heavy snow.

Special topography, diverse climate and complicated soil make Mount Emei a natural park of wildlife. There are more than 3,200 species of plants in the mountain, accounting for one tenth of the total identified in China. Of them, more than 100 are unique to Mount Emei or were first found here and thus named after the mountain. More than 2,300 species of wildlife live in the mountain, and 157 are rare or endangered species or species unique to the mountain. For example, the lappet butterfly that looks quite like a dead leaf, the giant panda and the lesser panda, and also the most well known monkeys. Most monkeys are not afraid of people, and they sometimes would bully tourists. Mount Emei also has the plants left over from 60,000 or 70,000 years ago, such as dove trees, whose flowers look quite like doves and which are also called living plant fossils.

Of all the mountains, Mount Emei is reputed as the "most pretty." On the one hand, it has a beautiful shape when looked from afar and it has a delicate and gentle outline, which resembles the delicate eyebrows of a pretty woman. On the other hand, the mountain is covered by forests, which add to its beauty.

Sunrise, sea of clouds, Buddha's halo and sacred lamps are four strange scenes on the Golden Summit. When sacred lights come out, the mountain peak is decorated with sporadic light spots, which flash and dance in ever changing manners. In fact, they are phosphorescent lights. However, monks in ancient times said that they were sacred lamps of Buddhism. When it becomes clear following a rainfall after noontime,

170

one can see rings of rainbow one or two meters in diameter from the clouds when looking down from the peak. People can see their own reflections in the rings, which reflect their actions like a mirror. What is even more fantastic is the fact that when hundreds of people look down the peak, they will never see the reflections of others, but just themselves. They are called "Buddha's halo".

Buddha's halo can be seen on other mountains, but Mount Emei is the only place where Buddha's halo can appear in more than 80 days a year and last for quite a long time every time they appear. Scientific research reveals that it is a natural phenomenon because of the diffraction of light in the clouds, which can only appear when slanting sun is above the clouds and people stand on the mountaintop. When under the sun, people and the reflections of people form a straight line and then fall on the clouds, Buddha's halo appears. However, ancient people believed that Buddha's halo meant Samantabyadra, or the Buddhist Goddess of Universal Benevolence, was exposing her real face to people. It is said that once upon a time, Buddha Sakyamuni sent the goddess, one of his disciples, to give lecture on Buddhism in Mount Emei. Belief in Goddess of Universal Benevolence started to spread in the mountain in the 3rd century AD, according to historical records, and Mount Emei has been considered as a ritual site for the goddess ever since.

Taoism had found its way to Mount Emei much earlier than Buddhism. In the year 143 AD, a man named Zhang Ling established a sect of Taoism in Qingcheng Mountain not far from Mount Emei. Not long afterwards, Taoism found its way to Mount Emei, where it has coexisted with Buddhism for nearly 1,000 years. Buddhism became stronger in the years followed while Taoism declined and finally withdrew from Mount Emei in the 18th century.

When Buddhism was in its boom times, the entire mountain had as many as 170 large and small temples, and almost every peak had its own temples. Now there are still 29 temples in Mount Emei, and of them, Baoguo Temple and Wannian Temple are the most famous. Baoguo Temple is the entrance of Mount Emei and also the largest temple in the mountain. Wannian Temple houses a copper statue of Goddess of Universal Benevolence, which was cast in the year 980. The goddess, wearing a golden crown, rides on a white elephant whose four feet tread on four lotus flowers. The entire statue is 7,35 meters high and weighs 62 tons. It is surprisingly marvelous that no trace of welding can be found on it.

The Leshan Giant Buddha on Mount Lingyun east of Mount Emei is another valuable historical heritage left over by our forefathers. The giant Buddha was carved on the cliff of Mount Lingyun, at whose feet is where three rivers, the Minjiang, Daduhe and Qingyijiang, meet. The Buddha was carved in the hope of borrowing Buddhist holy power to harness the devastating flood. A local monk whose clerical name was Haitong initiated the project and spent 20 years begging for alms for the collection of the first sum of fund. The project started in the year 713 and lasted for 90 years.

The 71-meter-high Buddha can be seen a dozen kilometers away. The Buddha's head is 14.7 meters long and 10 meters wide; its ears, seven meters long each; its nose and eyebrows, 5.6 meters long, respectively; and its eyes, 3.3 meters long each. The shoulders measure 24 meters wide, and the instep, 8.5 meters wide, large enough for some 100 people to sit on.

The Giant Buddha is not only great in size, but also

delicately carved with clear lines. What is even more fantastic is an invisible drainage system within the body of the Buddha. In the shell-shaped hair buns, the collar, the veins and crease, arms and chest are invisible gutters. Holes are dug on the back of its ears and back. These gutters and holes function as drainage, moisture-proof and ventilation systems to protect the Buddha from being eroded.

A 13-storey wood structure tower was constructed to protect the Buddha from the attack of wind and rains. The tower was destroyed in a fire and holes to fix the poles to withstand the tower can still be seen on the body of Buddha and cliffs on both sides of the Buddha.

The Leshan Giant Buddha has weathered wind and rains in more than 1,000 years and is still there, facing the flowing rivers and listening to the evening drum and morning bell. UNESCO experts commented that Leshan Giant Buddha could compete with any rock carvings in the world such as Sphinx and Valleys of the Tombs of the Kings in the Nile Valley.

Mount Emei and Leshan Giant Buddha were inscribed on the UNESCO list of World Cultural Heritage in 1996.

170 "Buddha halos" are often seen from this cliff on the top of Mount Emei.

171 An aerial view of the Golden Summit, the top of Mount Emei.

171

172

173

172 Baoguo Temple is the entrance of Mount Emei and also the largest temple in the mountain.

173 Qingyin Pavilion. Pay attention to the streams, for whose beautiful sound the pavilion is famous.

174 The copper statue of the Goddess of Universal Benevolence in Wannian Temple, which was produced in the year 980. The goddess, wearing a golden crown, rides on a white elephant whose four feet tread on four lotus flowers. The statue is 7,35 meters high and weighs 62 tons.

175 A lantern displayed in a Buddhist temple on Mount Emei. Seven dragons and several hundred Buddha images are engraved on the lantern.

176 A sea of clouds, with snow-clad mountains in the background.

174

175

176

177

178

177 The giant Buddha in Leshan, the largest in the world.

178 Gilded Buddha statue of copper at Fuhu Temple (Crouching Tiger Temple) .

179 An aerial view of the giant Buddha.

180 A foot of the giant Buddha. The instep is 11 meters long and 8.5 meters wide.

179

180

The Ancient City of Pingyao

How did a Chinese town look like hundreds of years ago? You'll see it for yourself once you are in Pingyao Town in Shanxi Province, north China.

The town dates back to 2,700 years ago, and has been the seat of a county government since 221 BC. The town we see today is largely what it looked like during the Ming and Qing dynasties (1368-1911). Among those ancient Chinese towns, Pingyao is the best preserved - in fact the only one where the original layout and structures have remained basically intact.

The Pingyao town came to be inscribed on the UNESCO list of World Cultural Heritage in December 1992. The UNESCO World Heritage Committee described the town as an "outstanding example of Chinese Han cities in the Ming and Qing dynasties." The town, it said, has maintained all its characteristics and presents a complete picture of development in culture, society, economy and religion in the history of China.

The town was expanded in 1370 to its present size of 2. 25 square kilometers. Like most towns in areas inhabited by people of the Han ethnic group, Pingyao is walled, with a moat flowing round the wall. There are streets, lanes, government offices, shops and religious sites in the town. A bird's-eye-view of the town reveals that the town resembles a turtle in shape. In China, turtle is an auspicious animal, symbolizing longevity. The town was so designed in hope that it would be impregnable and therefore survive forever. The town wall has six gates, one in the south, one in the north, two in the east and two in the west. The south gate looks like the head of the "turtle". The north gate, the tail of the "turtle", is in the lowest part of the town, which used to serve as the outlet of flooding water drained off from inside the town. The gates in the east and west resemble the four legs of the "turtle". Immediately beyond these gates, in between the moat and the "inner wall", there is an "outer wall" designed to further strengthen the town's fortification.

In feudal China, stringent rules were enforced on the size of a city or a town according to its administrative status. For a county town like Pingyao, each side of the wall round it must not be longer than 1.5 kilometers. The side of Pingyao's town wall facing south, however, is two kilometers long, the length being required by the local terrain. The other three sides are exactly 1.5 kilometers long each. In ancient times, almost all Chinese cities and towns were walled. At present, such walls can still be seen in only four cities. Walls in three are no longer complete. Pingyao is the only place with its wall intact. The wall of Pingyao is 10 meters high, built with rammed earth with gray bricks neatly laid on its surface. It is three to six meters wide on the top, enough for six horses to gallop side by side. There is a terrace every 40 to 100 meters on the outer wall. On each terrace there stands a two-story watchtower. The upper part of the watchtower served as a battlement and the lower part was where military supplies were kept. There are altogether 3,000 embrasures and 72 watchtowers on the wall. The numbers were deliberately chosen out of respect for Chinese sage Confucius

181

(551-497 BC), who had 3,000 followers including 72 known for their academic or political achievements. A pavilion dedicated to the God of Literature stands at the southeast corner of the wall. Structures on the wall bear evidence to the old belief that military might and intellectual wisdom combined to ensure peace and prosperity to the country.

The South Street serves as the town's axis line. On either side of the street we find the town's most important structures and these structures are arranged in symmetrical order. The Temple of Confucius and the Temple of the Town God are on the left side, and the Temple of Martial Valor and the old county government office are on the right side. A tower, 18. 5 meters high, sits astride the town's axis line. It was and still is the town's landmark building.

Shops and workshops on the major streets still maintain their outlooks of the town's heyday from the 17th century to the 19th when the town was a thriving business center. The town at the time was famous in particular as home to China's richest dealers of dyes, who had branches in almost all parts of the country. It was also in Pingyao that the country's first private money house, Rishengchang, came into being in 1824. Together with other private money houses in Shaanxi, these were predecessors of China's banking industry.

The money house, Rishengchang, is on the West Street. By the second half of the 19th century, Pingyao had become the country's financial center. Of the 51 money houses operating across China at the time, 22 were in Pingyao - to be exact, on the West Street barely 400 meters long. These money houses had branches in hundreds of Chinese and foreign cities. They are still there - no longer in business, of course - those courtyards with the frontal part once reserved for business and the rear part, as offices and residential quarters.

With the money they had made, rich merchants in Pingyao built beautiful houses for themselves. All houses in Pingyao are walled compounds. In following the tradition of filial piety, the main room in a compound, in most cases a spacious, south-facing cave dwelling, was reserved for the most senior member of the family,[1] which is flanked by one-story housing structures built with bricks and tiles. Most compounds have two, three and even four courtyards, depending on the families' financial status and political influence. Families with just one courtyard would be looked down upon for being poor and insignificant. In larger courtyards, the structures are always decorated with wooden, brick and stone carvings, as well as colorful paintings. Carvings and paintings bearing auspicious designs are found everywhere — on walls, doors, windows and pillars. By a close examination of their themes, however, one may tell what the owner of a compound was - a trader, an official, a scholar or a farmer. In the county town of Pingyao, 3,797 compounds are counted. Of these, 400 are still in good shape.

Two temples at Pingyao, the Country-Guarding Temple and the Double-Forest Temple, are on the UNESCO list of World Cultural Heritage as extensions of the ancient county town.

Fifteen kilometers to the northeast of Pingyao Town, the Country-Guarding Temple was built in the period of Five Dynasties (907-960). The temple's main architecture, known as the Ten Thousand-Buddha Hall, is China's oldest wooden structure preserved to this day. What is even more miraculous is that the painted sculptures in the hall show no trace of repairs even though they are more than 1,000 years old.

The Double-Forest Temple, which lies six kilometers to the southwest of Pingyao town, is 1,400 years old. It is a treasure house of ancient Chinese art with 1,566 painted sculptures, the tallest being more than three meters in height and the shortest, just 30 centimeters. Most of these were built during the Ming Dynasty.

[1] Pingyao is on the fringe of the northwest China loess highlands, where cave dwellings are popular. While easy to build, such dwellings allow good ventilation while letting in sufficient sunshine, therefore cool in summer and warm in winter.

181 The wall that surrounds the ancient town. Pay attention to those watchtowers.

182 The Pingyao Town surrounded by an ancient wall that has remained intact.

182

183

184

183 A gateway through the wall that surrounds the town.

184 An aerial view of the ancient town. The street that cuts the town in the middle serves as the town's axis line.

185 The tower astride the axis line serves as town's landmark buildings.

186 Inside a typical walled compound in the ancient town.

187 Photo shows the office of China's first private money house, Rishengchang, which came into being in 1824.

185

186

187

188

189

188 Painted sculptures in the Country-Guarding Temple. These painted sculptures show no trace of repairs even though they are more than 1,000 years old.

189 The sculptures of Sakyamuni and his followers in the Country-Guarding Temple.

190 A painted sculpture of the Buddhist guardian god Weituo in the Double Forest Temple.

191 The Double Forest Temple has a collection of 1,566 painted sculptures built in the Ming Dynasty. Here is one, depicting the Buddhist Goddess of Mercy, cross-legged, sitting on a lotus flower-shaped throne on the sea.

192 The main architecture of the Country-Guarding Temple, the Ten Thousand-Buddha Hall, is China's oldest wooden structure preserved to this day.

191

190

192

Classical Gardens of Suzhou

Small stone bridges over gently flowing rivers and residential houses on the riverside combine to make Suzhou beautiful. But the real beauty is behind some far from being eye-catching gates hidden in deep alleys. Inside these gates are the most exquisite gardens in China. They are poetry itself.

The most representative of Suzhou gardens are Garden of the Humble Administrator, Lingering Garden, Garden of a Fisherman and Villa of Green. These were inscribed on the UNESCO list of World Cultural Heritage in 1997. In 2000, Canglang Pavilion Garden, Lion Forest Garden, Yipu Garden, Ouyuan Garden and Tuisi Garden were added to the list. All these gardens used to be owned by private citizens. The oldest is Canglang Pavilion Garden, which was built in the 11th century. The rest were constructed during the Ming (1368-1644) and Qing (1644-1911) dynasties, when garden construction peaked.

The classic Chinese garden is first of all a place to live, then a place to stroll around and then a place where one can enjoy the beauty of the garden. Hence, rocks, water surface, architecture, trees and flowers are indispensable elements in building a garden.

Suzhou is a part of the Yangtze River Delta, the "land of abundance" where rivers crisscross and lakes dot. The pleasant climate is favorable for the growth of flowers and trees, which are naturally important for gardens. Moreover, the area abounds in strange-shaped rocks, which can be easily assembled into artificial rockery of various shapes and sizes in the garden. Economic prosperity naturally nurtures culture. In the Ming and Qing dynasties, for example, Suzhou produced 60 *zhuangyuan*, scholars who emerged the best from the highest imperial examinations. No other place in the country was match for Suzhou in this regard. At the time, Suzhou was regarded as ``the most prosperous and romantic place in this world to live in". Suzhou was really an ideal place to build gardens. According to historical records, there were more than 300 gardens in Suzhou during the peak of garden construction.

Building good gardens of course needed money. But what was more important was the culture embodied in the garden. The tastes of the garden owner, who set the requirements, and the professional proficiency of the garden designer, were especially important. A saying goes: "A garden reflects the fine taste of its owner who is free of vulgar interests." Suzhou gardens' owners were officials, men of letters and rich merchants. Of the officials, those in retirement and those who had been dismissed from their posts made up the majority. Some owners were themselves men of letters or painters. Although some were merchants, they were after fine tastes. They either designed the gardens themselves or worked out design plans in collaboration with professional designers. In addition, outstanding garden designers were accomplished in arts.

Most of the gardens are in the back alleys of Suzhou City, neighboring whitewashed and black-tile residential houses. The gardens are walled, preventing worldly hubbubs from entering and keeping the exquisite beauty within. Garden gates usually look plaintive, as if telling the passers-by that the garden owners wanted to be nothing but a hermit. Pushing open the gate, one sees small bridges over ponds or flowing water, rocks, pavilions, winding paths, trees, flowers, etc. All this seems the miniature nature. So, Suzhou gardens are also called "nature in the city".

As a matter of fact, the gardens reflect the owners' ideas of leisure and being far from the world cares. Chinese intellectuals had a tradition of turning to nature and artistic

193

accomplishments to please themselves when in political disgrace or oblivion. This, for example, finds expression in the Returning to Pastoral Life House in Garden of the Humble Administrator. In Garden of a Fisherman, a tablet states outright: "I am going to be a fisherman." The name of Yipu Garden suggests it is a place to plant flowers and grass. Ouyuan Garden means the husband and wife retire to farming life in pair. Bai Juyi, a famed poet in the Tang Dynasty, made it clear that a small residence with a pond, bamboo groves, bridges, books, wine, songs and music was enough for a white-bearded man to live in leisurely and pleasantly until one's death.

Suzhou gardens are often private gardens affiliated to private mansions. The largest is Garden of the Humble Administrator, which covers 50,000 square meters, and the smallest is the Villa of Green, which covers 2,100 square meters. Although not very large, one feels that the seemingly multi-dimensional space offers one beautiful scenery after another as one strolls in the garden.

The region where Suzhou is located is not hilly or mountainous. Even if it was, the mountains or hills could not be incorporated into the gardens. So, artificial rockery was created, so that the garden owners could enjoy the pleasure brought by natural mountains and rivers while staying in the city. The beauty of the artificial rockery lies in the inter-relations between the main pieces and the secondary pieces and the high and low rocks. In some cases, earthen mounds are studded with rocks and in other cases, rocks that were laid together are covered with soil. Flowers and trees are planted on the mounds formed by rocks. Suzhou is on the Taihu Lake and Taihu rocks have ever been a favorite of the garden builders. The cold rocks seem to take on life after being arranged by the garden builders. In Lion Forest Garden, for example, the rolling rocks create an impression that there are peaks and canyons. When visitors happen to be separated by the rocks, they find it difficult to find each other among the maze created by the bristling rocks.

Water surface plays an important role in Suzhou gardens. In Garden of the Humble Administrator, for example, water surface accounts for three-fifths of the total area. It is more than a static big pond. Instead, water surface is shaped by mounds, bridges, corridors and pavilions. There are winding creeks and irregularly shaped ponds, which look natural.

Buildings in the gardens are ingeniously designed and laid out according to the garden owners' needs for strolling, entertaining guests or reading. Most of the houses, halls, pavilions and corridors are small and exquisite, full of vigor. The layout of the architecture in Lingering Garden is worth special mention. One who steps on a winding long corridor immediately enters the garden gate. Walking along the corridor for a while, one feels relaxed. Then come various kinds of architecture, which divide the garden into a few integral parts. In the middle section, rocks form screens and ponds. Buildings dominate the eastern part. In the west section, winding streams and luxuriant trees make one feel that one is in the wilderness.

In Suzhou gardens, one often sees outside trees or flowers framed by windows and mounds planted with a group of trees or orchid groves. These are meticulously designed by garden owners in order to bring about pictorial effects.

Although the gardens are small in size, they somehow reflect a sort of largeness through their layout. The Garden of a fisherman is an example in this regard. Covering an area not yet one-sixth of Garden of the Humble Administrator, it is so well laid out that there is garden within garden, scenery beyond scenery, which are well juxtaposed in a seemingly multi-dimensional space. The many houses and halls do not look crowded. The mounds and ponds are small but not cramped.

One can never expect to see through a garden at one glimpse. Often, a piece of artificial rockery, or a wall, or an architecture, or a grove of flowers not far from the entrance serves as a screen, which denies the visitor the privilege to see through the garden. The winding paths and corridors and such "screens" are found everywhere. So one, strolling in a garden, often doubts if one can still go along when suddenly the path or corridor leads one into a new scene. The Lingering Garden is the most representative in this regard.

Although the scenery of in a garden as a whole is limited, scenes change with one's steps, and the same scene changes with the seasons. The same pond can offer a visitor golden fish and lotus flowers when one sits quietly by it. However, the pond, when mingled with the surrounding scenery, turns into a picture. In Summer, one feels refreshing breeze sitting by the pond. In Autumn, one can enjoy pattering of the rain on the withered lotus leaves.

Every gateway and every window are frames of beautiful scenery. In this end, Suzhou gardens are more like painting scrolls. The gateways and windows serve as links between different section of a garden, helping strengthen the sense of space.

Some gardens make the best use of outside landscapes, a kind of "borrowing scenery". Canglang Pavilion Garden is a representative in this regard. Rocks are predominant within the garden. But through the 100 or so windows along the corridor, one sees water surface outside the garden. The rocks within and the water without complement to each other. In the morning and in the twilight, the misty water surface adds pastoral beauty to the garden.

In really understanding and appreciating Suzhou gardens, accomplishments and attainment in traditional Chinese culture are needed, because the gardens embody the quintessence of the traditional Chinese architecture, painting, poetry, calligraphy and engraving art.

The World Heritage Committee of the UNESCO says that no gardens in other places can better reflect the ideas of garden design than Suzhou gardens, which create a universe within a limited space. These gardens, constructed between the 16th and 18th centuries, reflect the profound conception of learning from nature but transcending nature.

194

193 The Guanyun Rock in Lingering Garden stands 6.5 meters high and is one of the four most famous rocks in Suzhou gardens.

194 A bird's-eye view of Tuisi Garden.

195

196

195 A part of the Garden of Humble Administrator.

196 A part of the Canglang Pavilion Garden.

197

198

197 A part of Tuisi Garden. Pay attention to the stone boat on the pond and the buildings on the bank.

198 A glimpse of Huanxiu Villa (Villa of Green), which is famous for rockeries.

199

200

201

199 Wangshi Garden (Garden of a Fisherman), small but beautiful.

200 This arch bridge of stone, in Wangshi Garden, is the smallest of its kind found in Suzhou gardens, so small that it is dubbed as "single-step bridge".

201 The ground of Suzhou gardens is often paved with pebbles and broken bricks that make up various patterns. Shown here is the pattern of Chinese flowering crabapple.

202 Inside a chamber in Wangshi Garden. Pay attention to the delicate carvings.

202

203

204

205

206

203 A window in Liuyuan Garden (Lingering Garden) . Pay attention to the scenery outside.

204 A vase-shaped door in Huanxiu Villa Garden. In the Chinese language, "vase" and "peace" are homonyms.

205 A glimpse of Yipu Garden, or the "gardener's garden". The garden was named such to express the owner's interest in gardening and desire for freedom from worldly matters.

206 A window in Wangshi Garden. Pay attention to the scenery outside.

207 Inside the Hall of Enjoyment over Pine Trees and Scenery in Wangshi Garden.

208 The Lion Forest Garden is noted for rockeries. Photo show the scenery seen through a rockery.

207

208

The Old Town of Lijiang

When one gets to Lijiang in Southwest China's Yunnan Province, one is not far away from the legendary Shangri-La.

In 1933, the word "Shangri-La" first appeared in the British novel *Disappearing Horizon*. It is a place owned by both deities and human beings, where people live harmoniously with nature. Author James Hilton's inspirations came from the southwest of China.

The ancient town of Lijiang originally was the only bazaar on the Yunnan-Tibet trade route. Construction of the town began about 800 years ago. In the centuries to follow, shops and stores were set up to line the town's streets, and caravans were to come and go. Today, many people of the 6, 000 or so households in the 3.8 square-meter town are still doing what their ancestors did — making bronze and silver ware, curing fur, keeping inns and shops.

Walking through the town, one immediately has the feel of its age-old simple beauty. The streets are paved with stone plates, which, though polished by treading, still feature their natural textures. The stone paving protected the streets from wearing by horse hoofs of the caravans and also offered local people convenience since it kept down dust in sunny days and prevent water puddles in rainy days. Today the stone paving has become worn by treading over the ages.

Unlike other ancient Chinese cities, there is no city wall girdling Lijiang. Besides, the town is void of the axis line on either side of which residential and other buildings are arranged in symmetric order. Ancient roads and country trails converge onto the town from all directions and incorporate into those branch alleys. The alleys, in turn, converge onto four main streets, which then open into a 500 square-meter square. This is the Square Street, the most prosperous market place in the past. The winding alleys and streets are lined with wooden-earth structures or wooden-brick-structured residential houses. The ancient Lijiang Town is thus naturally, peacefully and quietly laid out.

The most common layout of Lijiang's traditional courtyard is the so-called "three houses plus one screen wall" — the main house in the center, with two wing houses and a screen wall facing the main house. Each house has two three-room stories. The main room mostly faces the south, which is for the most senior members of the family. The two secondary houses in the east and west wing are for the younger generation. Another type of layout is also popular. It consists of one main room, two wing rooms and one "lower room" facing the main room, which combine to make a quadrangle courtyard. Beside the yard in the center, there is a smaller yard at each corner of the courtyard. This kind of courtyard is called "quadrangle plus four yards." The floor of the courtyard is paved with pebbles or colorful stones, which make up various kinds of auspicious patterns.

If the ancient roads and residential houses lend simple beauty and a sense of remoteness to Lijiang, the surrounding snow-capped mountains and the gurgling creeks running through the town help shorten the distance between Man and nature. One easily sees the Jade Dragon Snow Mountain standing majestically outside the town, with the peak covered with snow all the year round. The chilly water from the thawing snow flows down the mountain slope, picking up spring water on the way. Three main water flows divide into numerous branches, which run along streets in the town. Some even flow through the courtyard walls, continuing their journey after greeting the courtyard residents. The widest stream running through the town is three or five meters wide and the narrowest, barely one meter wide. Although not deep, the crystal streams flow energetically, looking brimming the

209

banks. Pleasant gurgling is heard everywhere in Lijiang, especially at night, making people feel that they live by mountain springs. Water lends inspiring rhythm to the town and makes people feel purified and far away from worldly cares.

The ancient streets, small bridges and the streams represent the exterior appearance of Lijiang. The people, however, represent the soul of the town.

The majority of the residents in Lijiang belong to the Naxi ethnic group. Their ancestors worshipped nature, regarding quite a number of birds and animals as divine things. Legend has it that Man and the deity "Shu" were half brothers. Shu had the responsibility of overseeing mountains, forests, rivers, lakes and wildlife. At first, the brothers got along well with each other. But later, Man's greed led to destruction of forests, contamination of river fountainheads and killing of animals. Shu was very angry and decided to punish Man, hence, illness, floods, and earthquakes in the world. So, the Naxi people hold rites every year to offer sacrifices to Shu, praying for fortune and keeping away disasters.

Shu is believed to live near the fountainhead of rivers. So, the Naxi people forbid pollution of the water sources and felling of trees there, and even forbid making noises near water sources. In Lijiang, stone tablets inscribed with rules asking people to treat mountains, trees and water well are seen everywhere.

There are many wells in the ancient town. It is very common that one well is made up by three "sub-wells" separately for drinking, rinsing and washing. Small bowls are arranged by some wells for passers-by to get water themselves. Local people are in the habit of washing the streets. In the past, after trading on the bazaar ended for the day, people would dam the waterways and water would naturally flow into the Square Street and nearby alleys. Although this kind of organized street-washing activity has become history, local people are still getting water from the streams and washing the part of the street in front of their own houses. As a result, the streets in Lijiang are forever clean, especially in the morning.

In the Naxi family, women are in charge of family affairs and men are in leisure. The women are busy all the year round, doing heavy work, and seem never to rest until they are old. Only now, can they lean against the wall, bathing in the sun. The embroidered cape over their shoulders seems to be a symbol of shouldering the heavy duties. They, however, take all this easy, looking simple and peaceful as if the years have never made a stamp on their lives.

In contrast, many of the leisurely men are well versed in poetry, calligraphy, painting and music. What is important to them seems to inherit, play up and hand down the traditional culture. Naxi classic music is heard everywhere in Lijiang. Every village in the countryside has a traditional music band. The traditional Naxi music is considered living fossil of the ancient music because it reserves the musical forms hundreds of years ago, or even more than 1,000 years ago. These musical forms have long got lost in the rest parts of the country.

Men, however, do not monopolize the pleasant and gentle-paced life. A flower fair is organized each year in Lijiang. At the time, families display their best potted flowers and artificial rockery, sharing with each other the beauty. Local people grow flowers in their courtyards, which is the life-long hobby for many. Family members often get together in the flower-rich courtyard, sipping tea and chatting, whiling away time agreeably. Feasting party is also part of the pleasant life style in Lijiang. Relatives and friends organize feasting clubs, and dinners are regularly arranged by families in rotation to treat club members. Sometimes, the feasting takes the form of picnic. Money is pooled by the club members but cooking is done by one family each time. Women often play a leading role in this kind of activities. A conversation between a foreign reporter and a local old man was once recorded. The reporter asked the old man if the pace of life in Lijiang was too slow. The old man replied: "Why one should rush since everyone begins to head for the end of life the moment one is born."

The Naxi people have their own culture: Dongba Culture. It covers the Dongba writing system, Dongba scripts, Dongba Painting, Dongba music, Dongba dance, Dongba sacrificial rites. Dongba in Naxi language means "the Sage" or "the Master". The Naxi sages and masters inherit the ethnic group's ancient culture and hand it down to the younger generation. They are well versed in Dongba pictography and scripts. They are the elite of the Dongba Culture.

The Dongba characters are the only living pictography in the world today. It is universally admitted by the academicians that only the Naxi people alone in this world have recorded their own history with volumes of picture-like characters over the centuries. Today, more than 20,000 volumes of Dongba scripts are still being kept extant in Chinese and Western libraries. These classics are the encyclopedia of the ancient Naxi society.

American scholar Joseph Locke is called "father of the Naxi studies". He lived the in the Lijiang area for 27 years, starting in 1923. In his last days, he wrote to a friend, saying, "I would rather die amidst the flowers of the Yulong Snow Mountain than die lonely on his deathbed in the hospital."

Lijiang is a place that can never be forgotten. In 1997, Lijiang was listed by the UNESO as a site of World Cultural Heritage.

210

209 A bird's-eye-view of the Square Street, the center of the town.

210 The Jade Spring Park, also known as the Black Dragon Pond. Beyond this largest park in the town are the rolling Jade Dragon Mountains that are capped in snow all the year round.

211 A riverside street in Lijiang.

212 "Bridges" such as these are found everywhere in the town.

211

212

213

214

213 A full view of the town, which is 3.8 square kilometers large and has more than 6,000 households.

214 Photo shows a typical walled compound in Lijiang Town, featuring a range of two-story buildings and a corridor.

215

215 A well in Lijiang with three openings. Water in the well is in fact spring water.

216

217

216 A centuries-old street in town.

217 The exterior of a typical Naxi compound. Pay attention to the old man in traditional ethnic Naxi costumes.

218

219

220

221

218 Lijiang murals incorporate the most salient features of different religions and different sects of the same religion. Shown in this picture is a mural in the Duhe Dajue Temple.

219 An orchestra of the ethnic Naxi's traditional music that dates back to many centuries ago.

220 A part of the mural in Dabaoji Temple. Murals are seen in a dozen temples in the town and surrounding villages.

221 The Naxi ethnic group's Dongba scripts are the only live pictography in the world.

The Summer Palace

The Summer Palace in Beijing was an imperial garden of the Qing, China's last feudal dynasty. It is situated in the northwestern edge of the rapidly expanding city, though it was on the city's outskirts a few decades ago.

Before the Summer Palace was built, the imperial family had already had an imperial garden — the Garden of Perfect Splendor, which was recognized as the most beautiful, most magnificent garden in the world at the time. In 1774, Emperor Qianlong told his posterity in his Essay on the Garden of Perfect Splendor that they must never abandon this imperial garden for new ones in order not to waste the society's resources. But a few years afterwards, this emperor went back on his word and ordered construction of one more imperial garden — the Garden of Clear Ripples, the predecessor of the Summer Palace.

Emperor Qianlong was the fourth ruler of the Qing Dynasty. During his reign, China enjoyed economic prosperity and social stability. He made six tours of areas south of the Yangtze River, the most prosperous, most picturesque parts of China. While there, his majesty fell in love with those private gardens, and felt that none of the imperial gardens in Beijing was able to match them in beauty and layout. So he personally chose a place at the foot of the West Hill (Fragrance Hill) for a new imperial garden which, with a lake and natural hills, suited his artistic taste.

In 1750, Emperor Qianlong assembled the best garden designers, architects and artisans from across the country and earmarked one-seventh of the state revenue of the year for construction of the Garden of Clear Ripples, allegedly for water control and for celebrating the birthday of the queen mother. Construction of the garden was completed in 1764. But in 1860, the invading British-French troops burnt down both the Garden of Perfect Splendor and the Garden of Clear Ripples. Empress Dowager Cixi, China's de facto ruler during the last decades of the Qing, decided in 1888 to rebuild the Garden of Clear Ripples and renamed it "Garden of Harmony", which was to become known in the West as the Summer Palace.

The Summer Palace covers an area of 290 hectares, of which three-fourths is water surface. The complex comprises office quarters, imperial living quarters and scenery areas.

The office quarters are situated in the east of the garden. The main hall, the Hall of Benevolence and Longevity, is flanked by two rows of rooms for court officials on duty.

The imperial living quarters are behind the office area. Walking past the Hall of Benevolence and Longevity, one sees the Hall of Jade Ripples, which used to be the office of Emperor Qianlong in the garden but was later converted into the living quarters of Emperor Guangxu. It is here that Emperor Guangxu spent his last years under house arrest, which came after Empress Dowager Cixi got the upper hand over him in power struggle. Then comes the Hall of Fragrant Grass, the living quarters of the queen. Behind the hall there stands the Hall of Joyful Longevity, where Empress Dowager Cixi lived. In her last years, the Empress Dowager lived in the Summer Palace from April to October each year to while away the hot Summer. The Hall of Joyful Longevity has the best convenience in the Summer Palace, with an open-air imperial theater and the Long Corridor just a few steps away.

The Chinese think that the best gardens are those embodying the quintessence of natural landscapes and harmonizing what is artificial and what is natural. The area

222

where the Summer Palace is situated abounded in springs and boasted a vast water surface. Builders first expanded the area of Wongshan Lake and then merged all the lakes, pools and ponds of various sizes into one large lake, which was to be named the Kunming Lake. Then a long dike was constructed across the lake to dam back the water and raise the water level. The earth from digging of the lake was used to increase the size of the Wonshan Hill to be renamed the Longevity Hill in celebration of Empress Dowager Cixi's 60th birthday.

The Pavilion of Buddha Fragrance atop the Longevity Hill serves as the landmark of the Summer Palace. It stands 41 meters high and is magnificently decorated. When one climbs up the hill overlooking the Kunming Lake, one's eyes take in the lake, the West Hill and the pagoda atop the West Hill a dozen kilometers away. The pagoda and the hill are reflected on the lake, which combine to express the picturesque conceptions of the traditional Chinese landscape painting.

The lake is a perfect model of traditional Chinese garden building, which calls for making the best use of the surroundings to ensure a perfect harmony between artificial creation and natural landscapes. In the west of the lake, a long dike divides the water surface into three parts on which there are three isles, symbolizing the three fairy islands on the high seas where immortals are believed to dwell. At the foot of the Longevity Hill, the 728-meter-long corridor winds along the shore of the Kunming Lake. Taking a stroll along this, the longest corridor in the world, one can enjoy the lake and the hill immediately beyond in the south, as well as those gardens and courtyards at the foot of the hill. The Long Corridor not only shelters people from rain and the sun but also presents itself as the longest "art gallery" in the world, its beams painted with colorful pictures, mostly episodes of traditional opera pieces or landscapes.

Behind the Longevity Hill one finds himself in a world of tranquility and peace, where Buddhist temple structures in either the Han or Tibetan style are seen amid lush-green woods. The area is only 50 meters from the garden wall and had no natural landscapes. But ancient builders dug a canal that winds along the foot of the hill and diverted water from Lake Kunming into it, and then built miniature hills with earth from digging of the canal. On either bank of a 300-meter section of the canal there is an array of shops in traditional architectural style. Here we are in the "Suzhou Street", modeled on those riverside commercial streets in Suzhou, to which Emperor Qianlong took a special liking.

Smaller gardens within a large garden constitute a salient feature of the Chinese gardening design. The Garden of Harmonious Delight in the Summer Palace is a good example. Emperor Qianlong ordered building of the garden after he returned from Wuxi, a scenic city on the south bank of the Yangtze River, where he was fascinated by a garden called "Ease of Mind". The Garden of Harmonious Delight, which is modeled on the Garden of Ease of Mind, is quite small and has pavilions and corridors beyond a lotus pond. There are five small bridges across the pond. Of these, one is named "Zhiyu" or "Knowing-the-Fish". The name originates from a well-known talk between two philosophers that took place about 2,000 years ago. "Look, how happy the fish are, swimming back and forth in the water!" exclaimed one of the philosophers, Zhuang Zhou. Hui Zi, the other philosopher, asked: "How do you know the fish are happy since you are not one of them?" Zhaung Zhou replied: "How do you know I don't know the fish are happy since you're not me? "More than 100 scenic spots are counted in the Summer Palace, which combine to represent a perfect combination of the imperial might and natural beauty. There are also 3,000 buildings in the garden, designed and built in such a way as to form an integral part of the overall landscape.

The Summer Palace, the largest and best-preserved imperial garden in the world, was inscribed on the UNESCO list of World Cultural Heritage in December 1998. Evaluating the cultural importance of the garden, a report of the UNESCO World Heritage Committee describes it as the "epitome of the ideas and practice of the Chinese garden construction." These ideas and practice, says the report, "have played a key role in promoting the development of the art of the Oriental garden building."

222 The Buddha Fragrance Pavilion, 41 meters high, is the landmark building of the Summer Palace. A five-meter-high Buddha figure used to be enshrined in the hall.

223 A glimpse of the Summer Palace.

223

224

225

225 The marble boat, known as Qingyan Fang, in the Summer Palace.

226 The Seventeen-Arch Bridge links the east section of the dike on the Kunming Lake with an isle on the southern part of the lake. The bridge is 150 meters long, with 544 stone lions carved on its railings.

227 The Jade Belt Bridge on the Kunming Lake.

228 The "shopping street" behind the Longevity Hill. The so-called street opened for "business" only when the emperor and his wives came for a stroll, with court ladies and eunuchs acting as traders and shoppers.

224 The Garden of Harmonious Delight in the Summer Palace, one the "gardens within the larger garden".

226

227

228

229

230

231

229 The Pavilion of the God of Literature. In ancient times, this Taoist deity was worshipped as the guardian for scholars.

230 A part of the Long Corridor, the longest in the world.

231 The north slope of the Longevity Hill features Buddhist buildings in Tibetan style.

232 The south slope of the Longevity Hill that faces the Kunming Lake, with a range of buildings arranged in symmetrical order at different heights.

232 ▶

The Temple of Heaven

Where is the world's largest architectural group designed for Heaven worshipping? It is in Beijing, China.

Why worshipping Heaven? Ancient Chinese thought Heaven took care of everything on earth and meted out fortune or misfortune to people. It could either bring good weather for the crops, happiness and peace to the world, or disasters, wars and epidemics. As a result, the Chinese began worshipping Heaven more than 3,000 years ago. Taking advantage of people's awe and respect for Heaven, emperors called themselves "the Son of Heaven", claiming they had the divine mandate to rule the country. So, venues of Heaven worshipping were set up in capitals of all dynasties. It was also made known that worshipping of Heaven was the exclusive right of the emperor.

The Temple of Heaven we see today on the southern fringe of the city was the venue where the Ming (1368-1644) and Qing (1644-1911) emperors held Heaven-worshipping rituals and praying for favorable weather and bumper harvests. It was constructed in 1420. In the beginning, it was named "the Temple of Heaven and Earth" because the worshipping rites for Heaven and Earth were combined into one. In 1530, Emperor Jiajing of the Ming decided that the worshipping rites for Heaven and Earth be separated and instructed that temples for worshipping the Earth, the Sun and the Moon be constructed on Beijing's northern, eastern and western edges. At the same time, the Temples of Heaven and Earth was revamped and expanded and renamed the Temple of Heaven. Later, the Qing emperors made changes to the temple time and again, but the basic layout remained intact.

The area covered by the Temple of Heaven is roughly square. The two corners of the square in the south are in right angles while those in the north are in curves, representing the ancient Chinese idea of the universe - "Round Heaven, Square Earth". It covers 27,300 square meters, about four times as large as the Forbidden City. However, architecture is rather sparse in such a large area covered by luxuriant vegetation. The whole compound is laced by double walls. The area within the inner wall is called the "inner temple" and the area in between the two walls is called the "outer temple". The main buildings of the Temple of Heaven are in the inner circle and are lined up along a north-south axis. At the southern end is the terraced Huanqiu, or Altar of Heaven, and at the northern end, the Altar for Prayer for Harvests.

The Altar of Heaven is the most important structure in the Temple of Heaven. It was the venue where imperial Heaven-worshipping rites were held. In the center is the circular terrace of stone, standing five meters high with three planes. No roof was constructed to cover the terrace because the emperors offered sacrifices and paid respect skyward. In the center of the terrace is a circular stone plate with its diameter barely one meter. It is called Heavenly Heart Stone. Even a person whispers standing on the stone, the sound is echoed back as if many people were answering him. So the place is also known as "Millions Behind," meaning that the emperor had the support of the entire Chinese population when he was worshipping Heaven.

The surroundings of the terrace are solemn and quiet. The grand Heaven-worshipping ritual was staged at the dawn of every Winter Solstice, and the emperor would personally read out the eulogy. By then, lanterns were hung on the poles in front of the altar. Wisps of smoke issued out from incense burners, supposedly to reach the deities in the sky. Sacrifices were burned on a dozen pots lined up in the southeast. All this, amidst Heaven-worshipping music, combined to create an atmosphere of mystique.

To the north of the Altar of Heaven is a circular courtyard,

233

in the center of which stands the circular Huangqiongyu, or the Imperial Vault of Heaven, which is flanked by eastern and western side halls. This is the place where divine tablets for Heaven worshipping were kept when there were no worshipping rituals. The courtyard is walled. When two people, standing against the wall, speak to each other from afar, they hear each other clearly. Hence it is called "Sound-Echoing Wall." Round the very center of the hall's floor are fan-shaped stone plates arranged in nine circles. The inner most circle is composed of eight stone plates and the number of stone plates in each circle multiples at geometric progression. So there are 360 pieces in all. The number "eight" represents the "eight directions" — east, south, west, north, northeast, northwest, southeast and southwest.

Getting out of the north gate of the courtyard of the Imperial Vault of Heaven, one steps on a brick pathway that link up the Altar of Heaven and the Altar of Prayer for Harvests. The pathway, 360 meters long and 29.4 meters wide, is called Danbiqiao, literally Red Stairway Bridge. The road rises gradually from south to north, implying the long road leading up to Heaven. It is divided into three lanes. In the middle there is the so-called "Divine Road", which was for the deities to walk on. The lane in the east is the "Imperial Road", which was reserved for the emperor. The lane in the west is "Lords Road" for the nobility and court officials.

At the end of the pathway stands the Altar of Prayer for Harvests. The Qinian Hall, literally the Hall of Prayer for Bumper Harvest Years, is the most beautiful building in the Temple of Heaven. The hall sits on a huge triple-plane circular stone foundation. It stands 38 meters high and has three circular roofs of blue glazed tiles on three different planes. Both its interior and exterior are elaborately decorated. It is regarded as a masterpiece of the traditional Chinese wooden-structure architecture.

In addition, there are supporting structures in the Temple of Heaven, which are all in neat groups. These include the Imperial Fast Hall, where the emperor stayed and did fasting on the eve of the worshipping rites, as well as a place where sacrificial animals were kept and the Divine Music Agency where palatial musicians lived.

How did the architects of the temple manage to meet the double functions of the Temple of Heaven — worshipping Heaven and praying for bumper harvests across the country?

First, square and circular shapes were abundantly applied because the ancient Chinese believed that Heaven was round and Earth was square. Whereas the general layout is concerned, the walls in the north of the temple take on a curved shape, representing the round sky above. And the walls in the southern end have right angles, representing the square earth below the sky. The three main buildings, namely, the Altar of Heaven, the Imperial Vault of Heaven and the Altar of Prayer for Harvests, are all in circular shapes.

Numbers with highly symbolic meanings play a significant role in the construction of the temple. The ancient Chinese believed that everything under the sun was divided into two basic categories — *yin* and *yang*, namely, the negative and the positive. Heaven, the emperor and the odd numbers represented the *yang* and the number "nine" was the highest of the *yang* numbers. Ancient Chinese often used "the ninth sky" to mean the highest skies where the Heavenly Emperor, the supreme ruler of the universe, lived. As a result, the number "nine" is abundantly used in the construction of the Temple of Heaven. On the upper most terrace of the Altar of Heaven, for example, is a circular stone piece surrounded by circles of stone pieces. The number of the stones in the inner most circle is nine and the number for the circle immediately beyond it is 18 (9 multiplied by 2) and so on and so forth until the number for the outermost circle reaches

81. The three stone stair cases leading from the bottom terrace to the third terrace all have nine stone steps. The Hall of Prayer for Bumper Harvest Years has different functions from those of the Altar of Heaven. So the numbers there are mostly related to agriculture and seasons. The 28 wooden pillars of the hall are divided into three layers. The 12 pillars supporting the first roof symbolize the 12 hours of the day (in ancient China, one day was divided into 12 hours). The 12 pillars in the middle ring support the middle roof and symbolize the 12 months of the year. The numbers in the outer and middle rings add up to 24, symbolizing the 24 solar terms in the Chinese lunar calendar. The four pillars in the inner circle represent the four seasons of a year.

The Temple of Heaven also stands out with its colors. Yellow represents the earth and blue, the sky. So blue color is abundantly used in the buildings of the temple. Roofs of the Imperial Vault of Heaven and Hall of Prayer for Bumper Harvest Years, for example, are covered with blue glazed tiles. It is also true of the roofs of some walls and side halls. There are 60,000 cypress trees in the temple, of which more than 4,000 are at least 100 years old. The evergreen trees, the white marble steps, terraces and railings, blue roofs and the blue sky combine to create a solemn, holy and noble atmosphere.

In 1998, the Temple of Heaven was inscribed on the UNESCO list of World Cultural Heritage. The UNESCO affirmed the value of the temple in three respects. First, the Temple of Heaven is a masterpiece in both architectural and landscape designing. The temple plainly and yet strongly expresses some very important concepts of the universe, which exerted great influence on the development of one of the world's greatest civilizations. Second, for centuries, the unique design and layout of the Temple of Heaven have had profound influences on the architecture and planning in the Far East. Third, the Temple of Heaven symbolizes the "legitimacy" of the Chinese monarchy that rule China for more than 2,000 years.

234

233 The Hall of Prayer for Good Harvest after rain. This is the landmark building for the Temple of Heaven.

234 A full view of the Hall of Prayer for Good Harvest, a structure 31 meters high that stands on a three-story terraced platform.

235

235 All the main buildings in the Temple of Heaven are arranged in symmetrical order, sitting astride the south-north axis line that cuts through the complex in the middle. At the southern end of the axis line is the Altar of Heaven, where rites of Heaven worshipping were held every year.

236 At the northern end of the axis line is the Alter of Prayer for Good Harvest. Pay attention to the wall round the alter that forms a neat square and the Hall of Prayer for Good Harvest, which is a round structure, representing what the ancient Chinese perceived of the universe — "Round Heaven, Square Earth".

237 Photo shows the Red Stairway Bridge, in fact a pathway that links the Altar of Heaven and the Alter of Prayer for Good Harvest.

238 There are 60,000 cypress trees in the Temple of Heaven, of which 4,000 are at least 100 years old. All the trees help create a kind of solemn and holy atmosphere called for by Heaven worshipping ceremonies.

236

237

238

239

240

241

239 The Hall of Abstinence is where emperors stayed for fasting before Heaven worshipping ceremonies.

240 Enshrined on the round stone terrace in the Hall of Prayer for Good Harvest is the imperial tablet dedicated to Heaven. The four gilded pillars in the center of the hall symbolize the four seasons.

241 Here we see the Imperial Vault of Heaven, and the "echoing wall" that surrounds it.

242 There are 28 pillars in the Hall of Prayer for Good Harvest, which form three circles. Pay attention to the elaborately decorated ceiling of the hall.

242 ▶

Mount Wuyi

In the north of Fujian Province, southeast China, Mount Wuyi is just 650 meters above sea level. This mountain is not very imposing and magnificent, but it is famous for a beautiful landscape, a long history and glorious culture.

If nature is compared to a painter, Mount Wuyi can then be regarded as the painter's masterpiece of watercolor. It took the painter, so to speak, several hundred million years to paint the background of red sandstone topography, arrange 36 peaks in different postures, cover them with trees and grass and bring in a winding stream like a jade ribbon to connect the peaks. When clouds and fog are evaperating among the green water and red sandstone mountain, when rare birds and butterflies are dancing in the tea groves under sunshine and when insects with a history of hundreds of millions of years are chirping, this painting becomes alive and presents to the world the miracle of nature.

Tourists or hermits who come to Mount Wuyi today, like the ancient Min ethnic people several thousand years ago or like famous geographer and traveller Xu Xiake several hundred years ago, may take a plain bamboo raft to float down the Nine-Twists Stream into this beautiful landscape painting, into what Taoists perceive as dwellings of immortals.

Floating along the winding water, the raft will take one zigzagging through colorful mountain peaks, and then one will have a thorough understanding of the curcuitousness of this mountain valley. Of the nine twists, every one has a landscape of its own. In some twists, the water is turbulent and stormy. In other twists, the water is so shallow that one can wade across them.

Looking up, one can once in a while see the coffins high up in the caves or crevice of the cliff by side of the stream. They are tombs of ancient Min ethnic group in Neolithic Age. These coffins resemble the shape of a boat and some even have oars. One of them is almost 4,000 years old and is the world's oldest coffin preserved to this day.

Why was a coffin made in the shape of a boat? Legend says that these boad-shaped coffins would be used as boats by gods to bring the souls of the dead to the paradise, and those planks, called "rainbow plank bridge", were planks used by the God of Mount Wuyi to make a bridge of the paradise when he invited his neighbors in the mountain to a feast in the Heaven. Archaeologists believe this custom of burial reflects the life of the ancient Min ethnic group by the rivers.

How did the ancient Min ethnic people raise the coffins 40 meters up the cliff and put them in the caves or crevices? We cannot find solutions in the boat-shaped coffins and planks, which are just witnesses to a long lost civilization. Not quite far away from the mountain is the ruins of an ancient city built in the first century, which demonstrates the glory of the civilization of the Minyue Ethnic Group, who were descendants of the ancient Min ethnic group. Although the palaces, towers and pavilions in the city have long gone and so have the residences of the kings and his aristocrats, we can still find the traces of the past glory of the city.

Mount Wuyi and its waters are miraculous. The coming of Taoism in the 8th century has shrouded the mountain and waters in an ambience of fairyland. Mount Wuyi is respected

243

in Taoism as a dwelling place of immortals. As a result, many places in the mountain are named with the word xian, meaning immortal, such as Xianyiting (Pavilion for Immortals to Play Chess), Yanxiantan (Alar for Immortals to Feast), Xianyouyan (Rock Once Toured by Immortals), Xianrenchuang (Bed for Immortals) and so on.

The mountain has a long history of Buddhism as well. Buddhism was introduced here also in the 8th century and was to enjoy a long period of boom after the 11th century. The Temple of Tianxin Yongle, literally Temple of Eternal Happiness, has a history of about 1,000 years and still attracts many believers today.

Mount Wuyi is also the cradle of what is known in the West as neo-Confucianism, which was developed on the basis of traditional Confucianism. This school of Confucianism or Confucian philosophy was the orthodox philosophy authorized by the imperial authorities in the various dynasties from the 13th to the 20th century. It had a great impact on every aspect of Chinese social life. Its influence had also reached South Asia and Southeast Asia and it was reputed as the "representative of South Asia Civilization." Zhu Xi, founder of the philosophy, came to study in Mount Wuyi at the age of 14, and then he stayed in Mount Wuyi for more than 50 years, writing books, establishing his own school of thought and giving lectures. He established the Ziyang Academy of Classic Learning and Kaoting Academy of Classic Learning. Many of his students became renowned scholars, who disseminated and developed the Confucian school of idealist philosophy. Mount Wuyi has also become a mountain famous for this school of philosophy.

Confucianism scholars, Buddhist and Taoist monks co-existed peacefully in this mountain. We could have imagined a scene of a peaceful evening, when, under the same moon, Taoist monks would be making pills of immortality on their stoves while Buddhist monks would be reciting Buddhist scriptures, and at the same time, Confucian scholars would be pacing the mountain trails thinking about some complicated problems about life.

Along the line of 27 degree northern latitude, most places in the world are desert with very few plants. Mount Wuyi is the only place on the same latitude with a stretch of well preserved subtropical virgin forest. So it has become a natural shelter for wildlife. The entire mountain has a total of 3,728 plant species and 5,110 animal species including such rare species as South China tiger, leopard, tufted deer and yellow belly tragopan. This mountain is also very rich in insects and has a total of 4,635 species of insects. It has as many as more than 200 different types of butterflies. The beautiful teinopalpus aureus is one of the most valuable butterflies in the world. Now there are only 12 specimen all over the world and 11 of them are from Mount Wuyi.

Of all the plants, Wuyi Yancha tea is the most famous. As early as in the Song Dynasty (960-1279), Wuyi Yancha tea had already become an article of tribute to the imperial court, which had established an imperial tea garden in Mount Wuyi to supervise the making of the tribute tea. Starting from the 17th century, Yancha tea began to be sold to Europe and the Americas.

The best type of Yancha tea is called Dahongpao (Big Red Gown). In early spring when tea trees just sprout, the trees are red all over as if they are wearing a big red gown when looked from afar. Thus the tea is so called. The only four tea trees of this kind left are more than 300 years old, and their production output is very limited. As a result, the limited tea the four trees produce is considered as very precious.

A unique tea etiquette has been established in the past 1,000 years. The local people have developed 27 different formalities in their tea drinking ceremony, which speaks volumes for the aesthetic taste of the ancient Chinese.

To date, there is no conclusion as to when Wuyi Yancha tea has started to be planted in the mountain. But it doesn't matter. As famous Tang Dynasty poet Fan Zhongyan did, we may believe that the tea was first planted by fairies in Mount Wuyi.

Mount Wuyi was listed as a site of world cultural and natural heritage in December 1996.

244

243 The Shaibu Crag, "shaibu" meaning "sunning the cloth". It is thus named because erosion by rain makes its outlook resemble huge pieces of cloth hung for sunning.

244 An aerial view of Mount Wuyi.

245 A cloud-shrouded peak on Mount Wuyi. The peak is named "Dengtianyou", meaning "ascending the sky for a visit".

246 The Peak of Fairies at the side of the Tow-Bend Stream that cuts through Mount Wuyi.

247 This butterfly belongs to an extremely rare species. Live butterflies of this species are seldom .

248 Mount Wuyi is known as the "paradise of birds, land of insects and kingdom of snakes" in description of a surpassing bio-diversity it boasts.

249 The Nine-Bend Stream zigzags through Mount Wuyi.

250 Rising 2,158 meters above sea level, Mount Huanggang, is the peak of the Wuyi Mountain Range. Mount Huanggang boasts the most complete, best preserved eco-system that characterizes subtropical forest zones.

249

247

248

250

251

252

251 Mount Wuyi used to be a holy shrine of Taoism. Here is the Taoist Tianyou Temple on Mount Wuyi.

252 The Wuyi Palace dates back to the mid-8th century. It is one of the six most important Taoist shrines.

253

254

255

256

253 More than 4,000 relics have been excavated from the ruins of the palace complex of the Kingdom of Minyue. Here is a tile-end left over from that period, the two characters meaning "a long, long life".

254 Photo shows ruins of the palace complex for the Kingdom of Minyue. The complex dates back to 2,355 years ago.

255 Photo shows Wuyi Academy of Learning started by Zhu Xi (1130-1279), a founder of what is known in the West as "neo-Confucianism". Zhu stayed here for ten years to teach.

256 Mount Wuyi is famous for the Yancha tea, which was an article of tribute to the imperial court. Photo shows the ruins of an imperial tea garden.

Dazu Rock Carvings

Grotto art of Northern China boomed for a long time in ancient times. The Mogao Grottoes in Gansu Province, northwest China, the Yungang Grottoes in Hebei, north China, and the Longmen Grottoes in Henan, central China are now on the UNESCO list of World Cultural Heritage. Beginning the mid-8th century, however, people in northern China ceased to build grottoes for worshipping of Buddhism. At about the same time, people in a placed called "Dazu" in southwest China began carving Buddhist images on mountain cliffs and, as time went by, what is known as "Dazu cliff carvings" pushed grotto art to its final glory.

Dazu, meaning "good harvest and great abundance", is a county under the jurisdiction of what is now Chongqing Municipality. In this "land of cliff carvings", 75 sites have been placed under state-level protection for their cultural importance. Altogether, more than 50,000 statues, mostly produced in the period of the Five Dynasties (907-960) and the Song Dynasty (960-1279), are counted there. Of these, more than 70 percent date back to the Song Dynasty. The most representative, most magnificent statues are carved on cliffs of the Beishan, Baoding, Nanshan, Shizhuan and Shimen mountains.

Grotto art found its way into China from India in the third century. Statues in the early grottoes, with Yungang Grottoes as the best representative, have facial looks of ethnic minorities in the north and bear resemblance to statues of India. As time went by, an integration of the Chinese and Indian cultures was observed in grotto art, of which the Longmen Grottoes are regarded as the most typical. In contrast, Dazu cliff carvings are purely Chinese in artistic style. Buddha images carved on cliffs here have the same facial looks and the same clothes as Chinese pilgrims. While "divine" enough to inspire awe and respect, they look so friendly and gentle.

Let us see how Avalokitesvara or the Buddhist Goddess of Mercy is depicted in Dazu cliff carvings. The oldest Buddhist scriptures depict Avalokitesvara as being neither masculine nor feminine. In China, however, it was transfigured into a goddess. In Dazu cliff carvings, in particular, she is depicted as a lady who looks so gentle, kind-hearted, graceful and pretty. One statue depicts her as a shy, delicate girl, as the "goddess of charm". Another has two companions, a handsome man and a pretty girl, forming an "ideal couple" in the mind's eye of many.

Buddhist gods and goddesses here all look peaceful and gentle. Few of them have their bodies exposed, many with thin underclothes to cover their chests or breasts, reminding viewers of those aesthetic conceptions and ethical values that were once prevalent in China.

Buddhist teachings in their original are, more often than not, beyond comprehension of even many believers. In Dazu cliff carvings we find a unique way of disseminating these teachings. Let's see a group of carvings that can be compared to serial pictures – zigzagged mountain trails, forests and, moreover, a man who whips a buffalo, then walks it and, finally, plays flute and has a nap on its back. The buffalo is unruly at the beginning, but gradually it turns submissive. The "serial pictures," 27 meters long, in fact tell the essence of Buddhist teachings. The harnessing of the buffalo is likened to the cultivation of a person's inner world. The person finds it difficult to do self-cultivation, gradually becomes fond of it and finally becomes aware of the essence of Buddhism and attains Buddhahood. This is a typical example of how Buddhist stories are told in Dazu cliff carvings, through depiction of people's daily life -- raising chickens, drinking wine, having fun, and singing and

257

dancing.

Buddhism emphasizes salvation of the soul. It advocates equality between people and stands against distinction in status between the ruler and the ruled, the master and the slave, and the parents and the child. However, being dutiful to the parents is the essence of traditional Chinese ethics, which immediately challenged Buddhism when it was first brought into China. In order to spread in the country, Buddhism gave way to traditional Chinese ethics and Chinese Buddhism has made it a rule that Buddhist followers must be filial to their parents and that the religion itself must be obedient to the sovereign.

This theme finds expression in many cliff carvings in Dazu. Carvings in the Baoding Mountain depict in details the hardships parents suffer in bringing up their children, and what sons and daughters should do to fulfill their filial duties. Words are invariably inscribed side by side with such statues, telling people to be always indebted to the kindness of their parents. There are also statues depicting what people can do under the influence of alcohol – the father and son, the husband and wife, and the brother and sister fighting each other when drunken. Sakyamuni, founder of Buddhism, gave up his family for the salvation of the worldly people. In cliff carvings here, however, he is depicted as a filial son. He is seen tending his sick father and carrying his father's coffin. Underlining the Buddhist teaching of universal love, one carving shows Sakymuni feeding himself to a hungry tiger.

What would happen to undutiful children after they die? Dazu cliff carvings show them being struck by thunder and sent to the hell where they are fed with molten copper. Inscriptions that go along with these statues all have this to say: "Under all the 3,000 laws and decrees, being undutiful to one's parents is the greatest sin."

Buddhism is the main theme for cliff carvings in Dazu, but there are also carvings on themes of Confucianism and Taoism (China's indigenous religion). Here we find images of Taoist deities like the King of Hell, God of Thunder, Goddess of Lightning, God of Wind, God of Rain, etc. We also find statues of real persons who distinguished themselves in promoting Buddhism in the country. Those who sponsored the carvings invariably had their own images carved. Here in Dazu, differences between what is divine and what is human seem blurred. This phenomenon speaks volumes for the pluralistic religious belief in the Chinese folk culture. Figures of Buddhism, Taoism and Confucianism can be seen side by side with one another, without a clear distinction in status between them, testifying to an integration of the three philosophical systems, which is a salient feature of the Chinese culture.

The Baoding Mountain in Dazu was a holy shrine for the Mi or Esoteric sect of Chinese Buddhism, which features stringently organized religious rituals and chanting of incantations to drive away even spirits. Buddhist records suggest that the sect had its heyday in the Yellow River valley in the early eighth century, and found its way into Japan in the ninth century. Of the 51 carvings we find in the Baoding Mountain, half are based on teachings of the Mi sect. These were produced from the 9th century to the 13th, suggesting that the sect enjoyed a boom in Sichuan Province when it was declining in other parts of China.

As regards why human figures are often found along with statues of divine figures, a group of experts from the Dazu Cliff Carvings Museum gave an answer after a study tour of the Beishan Mountain in 1994. In the late Tang Dynasty, the experts concluded, many died in wars in China, and people had images of their dead relatives carved on the sacred cliffs in hope that their souls would be released from purgatory. In the period of the Five Dynasties, the Dazu area was in social turmoil, and people had their own figures carved to pray for peace and family reunion. In the Song Dynasty, a period of relative peace for this part of China, statues were produced in exchange for divine blessing. Few inscriptions indicate a desire for status and wealth in the worldly life.

Five sites, namely, the Beishan, Baoding, Nanshan, Shizhuan and Shimen in Dazu have entered the UNESCO list of World Cultural Heritage. The UNESCO World Heritage Committee gave the following comments: The steep hillsides of the Dazu area contain an exceptional series of cliff carvings dating from the 9th to the 13th century. They are remarkable for their aesthetic quality, their rich diversity of subject matter, both secular and religious, and the light that they shed on everyday life in China during this period. They provide outstanding evidence to the harmonious synthesis of Buddhism, Taoism and Confucianism in China.

258

259

257 This statue of Avalokitesvara holding a divine seal is found in Cave No. 136 on Mount Beishan. Beads "inlaid" on her crown remain largely intact even though the statue was built more than 800 years ago.

258 A full view of Dazu cliff, on which several thousand carvings, done over a period of 70 years around 1174, were counted on its face about 500 meters in length.

259 These statues in Cave No. 136 on Mount Beishan look elegant and are very Chinese. They are among the best pieces left over from the Song Dynasty.

260

261

262

260 The statue of Avalokitesvara in Cave No. 136 on Mount Beishan holds a precious pearl in her hands. It is also rated as a master art piece of the Song Dynasty.

261 A statue of Bodhisattva in Cave No. 19 on Mount Baoding. Pay attention to the background that features a beauty of simplicity in contrast to the peaceful smile on the face of Bodhisattva.

262 Photo shows Sakyamuni, founder of Buddhism, at the time of Nirvana (the Sanskrit for "liberation from existence") with a group of followers around. This group of carvings is found in Cave No. 11 on Mount Baoding.

263 This statue of Avalokitesvara, found in Cave No. 8 on Mount Baoding, has 1,007 arms, and each hand is inscribed with an eye while holding a religious object.

264 This group of carvings, found in Cave No. 20 on Mount Baoding, depicts those horrifying tortures inflicted in the hell on those who committed sins in their lifetime: knife-studded mountains they are forced to climb barefooted, cauldrons with boiling oil in which they are fried, etc.

263

264

265

265 A chicken-raising woman in Cave. No. 20 on Mount Baoding.

266 Rock carvings on Mount Shizhuan serve as evidence to integration of Buddhism, Taoism and Confucianism in ancient China. Here we see Confucius with some of his disciples in Cave No. 6 on Mount Shizhuan.

267 Carvings on Mount Shimen feature a co-existence of Buddhism and Taoism in ancient China. Picture shows a Taoist deity enshrined in Cave No. 10 on Mount Shimen.

268 This statue of Avalokitesvara is found in Cave No. 136 on Mount Beishan. Pay attention to the sun and moon in her raised hands.

266

267

Mount Qingcheng and the Dujiangyan Irrigation System

In the year 256 BC, King Zhao of the Qin State appointed Li Bing governor of Xishu or western Sichuan, southwest China. The appointment itself was of no significance in history. The governor, however, was to lead the building of a water control system that has gone down in history. This system, known as Dujiangyan, freed the Chengdu Plain from flooding once for all and turned the area into what is known in China as the "heavenly kingdom", a land of prosperity and abundance.

Flooding and drought were frequent occurrences on the Chengdu Plain before Li Bing came. The Minjiang River, the second longest tributary of the Yangtze River, often breached its dikes at Guanxian County, now Dujiangyan City, in Summer, flooding vast areas on both banks. The scourge went from bad to worse as sand and mud carried by the river in its water settled and raised the river bed. Moreover, Mount Yulei in the southwest of Guanxian blocked the river from flowing eastward. For this reason, areas east of Guanxian would suffer from drought while areas in the west were being flooded.

Shortly after he took up the post as governor of the area, Li Bing decided to harness the river. He relied on his son and the local people for the job. Instead of building a dam to contain the flood waters, they made the best use of the favorable topographic conditions and built a dike to divide the river midstream into two channels. The channel west of the fish-like dike, known as the Outer River, is in fact the mainstream of the Minjiang River, and was designed to divert flooding water. The channel east of the dike, or the Inner River, was to divert water for irrigation. The far end of the dike is called "Fish Mouth", which was so cleverly constructed that ever since the project was put to use, it has been capable of dividing the water volume according to a right proportion. In Spring, when the water flow is small and farmland is thirsty of water, 60 percent of the Minjiang River water will flow into the Inner River and only 40 percent into the Outer River. In the flooding season, the proportion will be the other way around: 60 percent of the water in the Minjiang River flows into the Outer river and 40 percent into the Inner River to prevent the farmland from being flooded.

At about 1,000 meters downstream, the Inner River reaches Baopingkou, the entrance of a 20 meter-wide tunnel dug through Mount Yulei. It was not easy to tunnel through the mountain before gunpowder was invented. Li Bing, however, was not to be daunted. Upon his order, workers heated rocks with fire to make them expand and, when they were hot enough, cold water was poured on them to make them contract and crack. The entrance of the tunnel can automatically adjust the volume of water from the Inner River. It diverts excess water from the river into the irrigation system.

While diverting flood waters in summer, the concave dike between the Fish Head and Baopingkou will wash sand

269

in the Inner River down into the Outer River, and is therefore called "Feishayan" (Sand Flying Dike). When water of the Inner River rises above its limit, the excess water will flow over the Sand Flying Dike into the Outer River along with the mud and sand in it, which would otherwise settle to silt the Inner River and Baopingkou channels. When a flood is devastating, the Sand Flying Dike will automatically collapse to allow flow of water from the Inner River back into a main tributary of the Minjiang River.

The principle for construction of the Dujiangyan Project is quite simple, but the wisdom it represents has won admiration from hydraulic experts 2,000 years after it was built. All the materials used in the project were locally available. The area is overgrown with bamboo. Bamboo slices were used to make cages to hold pebbles with, which were then used as construction materials. Numerous irrigation systems were built in ancient times in other countries – Nur-Mammurabi Canal on the Euphrates in Babylon and those canals in ancient Rome. However, these have long been deserted. In contrast, the Dujiangyan Water Control System is still used, to the benefit of millions.

Mount Qingcheng, 15 kilometers to the south of Dujiangyan, has been a holy shrine of Taoism, the indigenous religion of China, for well over 1,800 years. Pine, cypress, dawn redwood, nanmu and Chinese sweet gum in different shades of green cover this "green world" as the mountain is known. In those dense forests, on those cliffs and in those valleys, you can hear nothing but the whistling of wind and the singing of streams and birds, for which Mount Qingcheng has been fame as the "mountain of tranquility".

Possibly because of its tranquility, Mount Qingcheng was destined to become the birthplace of Taoism. In the year 143 AD, a man named Zhang Daoling came to Mount Qingcheng, where he built a simple hut on his own and began to propagate his doctrines that were to develop into Taoism. Believers of Taoism call Zhang Daoling "Heavenly Master", and Mount Qingcheng is therefore referred to as the "Heavenly Master's Mountain". Many sects of the religion are attributed to Mount Qingcheng, where their founders stayed for cultivation of their inner world. With support from the imperial court of the Tang Dynasty (618-907), Taoism prospered, and consequently, Mount Qingcheng became the religion's national center. During its heyday, it had more than 70 Taoist temples. About half of these buildings are still in good shape.

On Mount Wudang, another holy shrine for Taoism, in grandeur and magnificence, the palaces and temples are quite similar to imperial palace buildings. In comparison, Taoist buildings on Mount Qingcheng are simple and plain, or more compatible with the doctrines of Taoism. Taoism, it is said, originates from teachings of Lao Zi, a Chinese philosopher who lived about 2,500 years ago. Lao Zi stood for a life free from worldly matters, for a life of peace and tranquility that blends with nature.

The Palace of Supreme Heaven on the highest peak of Mount Qingcheng is known not only as a holy shrine for Lao Zi but also for those simple, beautiful buildings there. The main gate, the archways and rails are all structures of stone and the main hall is wooden, with a visual impact strong enough to bring visitors back to ancient times when locally available materials had to be used in construction. Looking down from the temple after dark in Summer, people can see sporadic lights in the mountain, at one time just a few twinkling and at another, hundreds or thousands just like the star-studded sky. These lights, it is said, are "lamps" lit by the God of Mount Qingcheng. The true fact is that they are jack-o'-lanterns.

Mount Qingcheng and the Dujiangyan water control system were inscribed on the UNESCO list of World Cultural Heritage in November of 2000.

270

271

269 The gate tower at the foot of Mount Qingcheng.

270 A glimpse of the Dujiangyan Water Control System. Pay attention to the dike mid-stream that regulates the water volume for either irrigation or flood prevention.

271 Baopingkou, the entrance of a tunnel dug through Mount Yulei that diverts water from the Minjiang River for irrigation.

272

273

272 Photo shows the memorial temple in honor of Li Bing and his son.

273 The Chinese characters carved on this stone wall means "dredge the riverbed deep, and limit the height of the dike", summarizing Lin Bing's experiences in building the water control system. The wall is an important part of the Lin Bing and Son Memorial Temple.

274 The Dragon Taming Temple at Dujiangyan. A Taoist shrine, the temple is dedicated to Li Bing. Legend goes that Li Bing completed the project by subduing the dragon demon that had caused the droughts and flooding.

275 An aerial view of the Anlan suspension bridge. While on the bridge, one commands a full view of Dujiangyan.

276 A bridge on an ancient trail on the hill that overlooks Dujiangyan.

274

275

276

277

278

277 Mount Qingcheng, one of the earliest shrines of Taoism, features a range of Taoist structures hidden deep in forests.

278 The Temple of Superior Heaven, where Lao Zi, a philosopher who lived some 2,500 years ago, is worshipped as the supreme teacher of Taoism.

279 The Hall of Three Heavenly Superiors, where the highest-ranking Taoist gods are enshrined.

279

Longmen Grottoes

The Longmen Grottoes are built on two cliffs facing each other across the Yishui River, about 13 kilometers to the south of the center of Luoyang City, Henan Province, central China.

Luoyang was capital of nine dynasties in ancient China. In the year 493 AD, North Wei (386-543 AD), a political regime established by an ethnic minority group in North China, moved its capital to Luoyang. The North Wei imperial family had already built grottoes for worshipping of Buddhism near its old capital, what is now Datong of Hebei Province, north China. In Luoyang, building of grottoes was resumed, and continued for several hundred years in North Wei and some of the following dynasties.

Altogether, 2,345 caves are counted on the cliffs, in which there are more than 100,000 statues. Large-scale building lasted for more than 150 years from the North Wei to the Tang Dynasty (618-907). About 30 percent of the caves were dug in the North Wei Dynasty, 60 percent in the Tang Dynasty, and the rest 10 percent, in some of the following dynasties.

In the 40 years when Luoyang was the capital of the North Wei Dynasty, a dozen caves were dug. Of these, the Guyang and Binyang grottoes are the best known.

The Guyang grotto was the earliest built in Luoyang. Three Buddha statues are found in the cave. The main Buddha, 6.12 meters high, is placed in the middle, in front of the south-facing wall, and is flanked by the other two. According to historical records, the cave was dug with donations from the North Wei imperial family and court officials. The main Buddha looks a bit emaciated though with an elegant bearing, which is quite different from other Buddha statues built in the same period. Scholars say that it may have modeled after the image of Emperor Xiaowen of the North Wei Dynasty.

The three statues seem exceptionally imposing relative to the other statues in the cave. This is because when the full ceiling of the cave were carved with Buddhist images, workers dug the floor several meters deep and opened up the middle and lower layers of niches. These niches in different sizes are beautiful in shape, and the upper part of the niches as well as the Buddha images are delicately carved with varying decoration designs. Of these, a series of small statues telling the story of Sakyamuni from his birth to his attainment of Buddhahood was recognized as representing the acme of the sculpture art for the North Wei Dynasty.

Immediately after the Guyang Grotto was dug, work began on Binyang. The building began in the year 500 and lasted for 24 years. Three caves had been planned, but only the one in the middle was finished because of court turmoil. The other two caves respectively in the north and south were dug in following dynasties. This central cave is, in fact, a large Buddhist palace or temple. A complete set of Buddhist statues were carved in the cave and they look splendid while some light color makes the cave look elegant as well.

The Buddhist palace cave is culturally important because it marked completion of the change of grotto art from something purely Indian to a part of the Chinese culture. In addition, the dress style and bearing of the statues that had been learned from south China had finally taken shape in the statues in this cave palace. The characteristics of the dress style of the statues in Yungang Grottoes can still find expression in the statue of Sakyamuni in the upper shrine inside the Guyang cave. The dress style and shapes of the statues on the second shelf are quite different, and they belong to the style of South China called "xiugu qingxiang"(meaning graceful in bones and delicate in facial expression). This can

280

find expression in the main Buddha statue in the Binyang cave, which, in the loose costume of the Han ethnic, looks elegant and graceful, with corners of his mouth turning a bit upward and a smile on his face. This statue gives the impression that the distance between what is divine and what is human is narrowed down. It needs to be noted that statues built earlier in Yungang Grottoes look quite dignified and awe-inspiring with big, strong bodies, reflecting the valiant disposition of northern ethnic groups.

Changes in grotto art reflected development of the society at the time. Emperor Xiaowen moved the capital to Luoyang because he wanted his nation to learn from the advanced culture of the Han ethnic group. Under this emperor, the political system of the dynasty was restructured by modeling after the political system of the ethnic Hans, and ethnic minority people were encouraged to speak the Han Chinese, wear ethnic Han clothes and study Confucianism. These changes in policy are discernible in statues in Longmen Grottoes.

Feudalism had its heyday in the Tang Dynasty. The prosperity China enjoyed at the time pushed the ancient Chinese culture and art to a new high and added glory to Longmen Grottoes.

From 650 to 704, Emperor Gaozong and his queen, Wu Zetian, were in power in succession. Both were devoted believers of Buddhism. The emperor came to Luoyang for the first time in the year 657, and made the city the east capital of the Tang Empire. The sole female monarch in the Chinese history, Wu Zetian stayed in Luoyang for 49 years and, under her reign, the city served as the country's de facto political center. Naturally Longmen became the place for Buddha worshipping by the imperial family and aristocrats.

Thirty-five large grottoes at Longmen date back to the Tang Dynasty, including seven that were renovated on the basis of caves dug in previous dynasties. There are many smaller caves of the Tang Dynasty, and some of them line up in groups. More often than not, several people pooled their money to have a cave dug, and then each would have a statue of his or her favorite god or goddess built in the cave.

The statue of Vairocana, the Sanskrit for "God of Light", is the most magnificent of all the statues built in the Tang Dynasty. It was built in the year 675, in a grotto temple called Fengxian. The God of Light, 17.14 meters tall, sits in the middle of a niche, with nine other Buddhist gods, all ten meters tall, in his company. This colossal Buddha has a broad forehead and beautiful eyes. He turns his lips slightly upward and he lowers his head a little bit. A faint smile makes him look like sagacious and benign middle-aged man, so charismatic as to inspire both awe and respect. Critics describe the statue as a perfect combination of what is the best in a man's physical appearance and inner world. Scholars believe the statue was modeled after Empress Wu Zetian and can therefore be considered her embodiment. This assertion is somewhat justified. In reality, Empress Wu Zetian earmarked a big sum of money from her private budget to fund the building of the grotto temple and the statue there. Moreover, she attended the ceremony to celebrate the opening of the grotto temple.

Statues in Wanfo cave and Qianxi and Kanjing cave temples are also among the best representatives of the Tang Dynasty's grotto art.

The Wanfo Cave has more than 15,000 Buddha sculptures, and many of them are just a few centimeters high. On the walls of the cave there are relieves depicting court musicians at work. The main Buddha statue in the Qianxi Temple is recognized as one of the most beautiful artworks left over from the Tang Dnasty at Longmen. Twenty-nine relieves on Buddhist themes are the major attraction at the Kanjing Temple.

The imperial family, aristocrats, merchants and even poor people were involved in the building of the Longmen Grottoes and those magnificent statues. Donors included foreign Buddhist believers as well. Back in the early 1950s, designers and artists working for the building of the Monument to the People's Heroes in the center of Tian'anmen Square, Beijing, repeatedly visited the Longmen Grottoes for inspiration. This is just one of the numerous facts testifying to the artistic value of the ancient artworks kept in Longmen Grottoes.

In addition to statues and relieves, we find in those caves 2, 800 inscriptions on who built this or that cave and for what, and when the project began and when it was completed. Many of these are excellent works of Chinese calligraphy. Among them, 20 are recognized as the most valuable pieces left over from the North Wei Dynasty, and 19 of these are found in the Guyang Cave.

The Longmen Grottoes are valued not only for their artistic importance. The statues and other artworks there tell us a lot about China's political, economic and social life more than a thousand years ago. They are in fact a museum of anything and everything in China at the time – religious beliefs, fine arts, architecture, calligraphy, music, fashion and medicine.

The Longmen Grottoes came to be inscribed on the UNESCO list of World Cultural Heritage in 2000.

281

282

280 Work on Binyang Middle Cave began in the year 500 AD. The main Buddha in the cave wears a loose gown of traditional Chinese style and has a smile on his face. In artistic style, statues in the cave are largely free from influence of Indian art.

281 A full view of the Longmen Grottoes.

282 Digging of the Lotus Cave started in 526. The cave features large, beautiful lotus flowers, the Buddhist logo, carved on its ceiling.

283 Inscriptions carved on stones at Longmen record the names of those who sponsored the digging of grottoes, along with the whens, hows and whys. Many of these inscriptions are excellent works of calligraphy.

284 Flying deities in Kanjing Temple. This cave temple dates back to the 8th century.

283

284

◀ 285

286

287

288

289

290

291

285 Fengxian Temple is the largest open-air Buddhist shrine at Longmen. Building of the cave temple was completed in 675. This statue of Buddha is 17.14 meters high and is rated as a best piece of China's grotto art.

286 These statues of Arhats or Buddhist guardian gods, 29 all told, are enshrined in Kanjing Temple built in the Tang Dynasty. They are 1.8 tall.

287 Buddha with some disciples and Bodhisattvas in Fengxian Temple.

288 The queen paying tribute to Buddha. Most relieves found in Shiku Temple depict Buddha worshipping by emperors and their wives.

289 Guyang Cave was the earliest of all dug at Longmen and has the largest collection of ancient art works. It is in fact the largest treasure house of sculptures built by emperors and aristocrats of the North Wei Dynasty.

290 Buddha with two Bodhisattvas enshrined in Binyang Middle Cave are recognized as representative of the aesthetic style prevalent in south China at the time.

291 Jinan Cave was dug during the last decade of the 7th century. Though no longer complete, statues of strongmen are regarded as among the best works of the Tang Dynasty.

Ancient Villages in Southern Anhui – Xidi and Hongcun

Over the past two decades, those ancient villages in southern Anhui Province, east China, have drawn increasing numbers of visitors from all over China and the world, who come to see what life looked like in the past.

From the 16th century to the early 20th when China was under two successive dynasties, the Ming and Qing, on those ancient roads we see in Huizhou today were mostly locals, those out for business or to study or take official posts. During those long centuries, Huizhou produced numerous merchants and traders, who left their hometown when very young and wouldn't return until they thought they had got rich enough.

Finally did they come back, with money to build residences of their own, in order to be neighbors of those picturesque rivers and mountains and, more importantly, to add glory to their ancestors. As time went by, the villages where they lived became known far and wide for their residences. The most representative of these villages are Xidi and Hongcun in Yixian County under the jurisdiction of Huizhou City.

In ancient China, households of the same bloodline often lived in compact communities in the same place. The village of Xidi is home to a clan named Hu. The village is more than 900 years old, dating back to the time when the clan's ancestors came to settle. Two streams flow through the village all the year round. The residences with white walls and black tiles are all connected. The most eye-catching are the walls, which are higher than the roofs to prevent flames from spreading to neighboring courtyards when one courtyard catches fire. They were also designed to prevent thieves from breaking in and protect courtyards from strong winds. Those high walls look like horses raising their heads, and they are thus called "horse-head walls".

Flanking a road paved with stone plates are narrow streets and lanes, with the horse-head walls blocking vision of strangers. Most of the residences have small windows, and it is said that business people here did not want to exhibit their wealth. The compounds have the same appearance, plain and simple. As a result, outsiders can hardly tell which family is wealthier.

Another scene unveils itself inside the courtyard of a residence. Brick-wooden chambers on three of the four sides of the courtyard surround an open patio that ensures ventilation and sunshine. Water from all chambers in the courtyard drains into the open patio. As the old saying goes, "one must never let rich water flow into others' fields", this symbolizes a resolve of the family to always keep its wealth for itself. The front chamber usually has three rooms. The room in the center is the largest and fitted with good furniture. In old times, it was the sitting room for male members of the family, and also the room where the most important guests were received. Most of the chambers are two-story structures. Such a design suits the old tradition that favors big families, families in which members of all generations live under the same roof. Residences of wealthy families may each have three or even more courtyards, and these courtyards are invariably connected.

Many courtyards here are garden-like, with gold fish ponds, plants and rockery. The ground is invariably paved with stone plates or pebbles, in such a way as to form auspicious designs and patterns. Carvings are found

292

everywhere in courtyards here, on doors, windows, rails, columns and roofs. Decorations like these vary in content and extent, depending on the financial status and political influence of the families.

The Hu Clan Hall, or the Ancestral Hall of the Hu Clan, is higher and larger than any other structures in the village. In old times, it was where members of the clan gathered to pay tribute to their ancestors and meetings were held for decisions on important clan affairs. It was also where disputes between clan members were mediated, and those having acted in violation of the clan rules were punished. In feudal China, ancestral temples were symbols of the clans' influence, wealth and glory. Branches of a clan may have ancestral halls of their own, provided these are smaller than the halls for the entire clans.

The Hu clan had its heyday from the 17th century to the 19th. During that period, a man named Hu Guansan became the sixth richest in southern China. He built the Hu Clan Hall and several residences in the village. Before his son married daughter of the prime minister, he had a huge tower built for reception of his relatives by the marriage. Also built was a hall for reception officials who were to come to offer greetings. Hu Gansan was just a most typical wealthy businessman from the village. The village of Xidi today has a population of more than 1,000 and 124 well-preserved residences. When at the peak of prosperity, it had as many as 600 residences, 34 ancestral halls, 99 streets and lanes for a population of nearly 10,000.

These residences are not symbols of wealth only. Businessmen from Huizhou were as reputed for education of their children as for wealth. As the old saying goes, "scholars are superior to people in all other walks of life" – in ancient China, officials were chosen from among scholars through state examinations. Wealthy businesspeople in Huizhou had enough wealth to build schools and invite the best teachers to teach their children. Altogether, 115 members of the Hu clan took official posts in the Ming and Qing dynasties, adding fame to their clan and households.

Scholars invariably dreamed of "becoming an official to work for the good the country". There are also those who, though rich, preferred to live a leisurely life, a life free from politics. This Xidi Village was as reputed for those scholar-gentry families as for those who were rich. The residence named Lufutang, or Mansion of Happy Experiences, belonged to a scholar-gentry family. It is still there, as aloof and elegant as its old owners who spent their lifetime reading, writing poems, doing paintings and collecting relics. Couplets left over from them testify the values they cherished, the likes of "Benevolence is the pursuit of a family centuries old; reading is the best one could dream of in this world".

About a dozen kilometers from Xidi, visitors find themselves in the picturesque Hongcun Village. For its beauty, Hongcun is known far and wide as a village that can only be found in traditional Chinese paintings.

The village, 800 years old, was home to the Wang clan, a most influential, most powerful clan in the area. A bird's-eye-view from above the village shows that in layout, the village looks like a water buffalo sleeping at the foot of a hill, with the hill resembling the head of the " buffalo", groves of trees forming the horns of the animal and clusters of residences, its body.

Once inside the village, one just can't help marveling those zigzagged streams flowing in front of every compound, which bring in water from springs far, far away. The streams converge into a half moon-shaped pond in the center of the village, and then branch out until emptying into a lake outside the village. The streams are called " intestines" of the "buffalo", and the lake, its belly. Water is diverted from the streams into compounds for drinking, washing, watering plants and raising ornamental fish.

The village still has more than 100 ancient buildings including residences, schools and ancestral halls. Most were constructed from the 14th to the 19th century. The largest and best decorated is the Chengzhi Mansion built by a salt merchant in 1855. The residence has nine patios, seven multi-story buildings, 136 columns, 60 gates and doors, 60 windows and, believe it or not, a place for angling. The most exquisite and elegant are those wood carvings, which were done by 20 artisans in four years. It is said that more than 3,000 grams of gold was used to decorate the carvings.

The villages of Xidi and Hongcun were inscribed on the UNESCO list of World Cultural Heritage in 2000.

293

294

292 The 800-year-old Xidi Village seen from outside.

293 A full view of Hongcun Village.

294 The villages of Xidi and Hongcun both feature lanes like this. The lanes are invariably narrow and paved with stone plates.

295 The exterior of a courtyard in the area.

295

296

297

296 All courtyards in Hongcun are found the semilunar pond in the center of the village.

297 Inside a courtyard in Xidi Village.

298 The lake adds beauty to Hongcun.

298

福
便宜多自吃虧来
快樂每從辛苦得
創業難守成難知難不難

299

300

299 Chengzhi Mansion in Hongcun built by a salt merchant in 1855.

300 Inside an ancient school in Hongcun.

301 A courtyard with a fish pond. The photo was taken in Hongcun.

301

Imperial Tombs of the Ming and Qing Dynasties

From the year 221 BC when the first Chinese emperor was enthroned until 1911 when the last emperor was dethroned, emperors of all dynasties advocated luxurious burials to demonstrate filial duties to the deceased. They regarded their own mausoleums as the palaces they were going to use after they died, and that is why imperial mausoleums preserved to this day are, without exception, large in size and look imposing.

In 2002, the Xianling Tomb of the Ming Dynasty (1368-1644) and the east and west imperial tombs of the Qing Dynasty (1644-1911) came to be inscribed on the UNESCO list of World Cultural Heritage.

In most cases, an imperial mausoleum is divided into two parts, the part on the ground and the part underground. The underground part, in fact an underground palace, was built with stone and bricks to accommodate the remains of the emperor, along with a range of burial objects the dead emperor was supposed to use in the nether world. Structures on the ground include the Divine Road that leads to the tomb, the mausoleum gate, palace halls, a pavilion that shelters a stone tablet dedicated to the dead emperor, and an array of stone human and animal statues supposedly serving as the dead emperor's guard of honor. The grandeur and magnificence of imperial mausoleums speak volumes of the supremacy of the Chinese sovereign.

Ancient Chinese were keen to "*feng shui*" or geomantic omens, believing that the location of a house or a tomb and the natural surroundings of the burial site were to influence the family's fortune and the future of the later generations. Such ideas find explicit expression in the sites of the imperial tombs of the Ming and Qing dynasties. The "*feng shui*" idea is certainly superstitious, but it embraces the traditional idea of harmony between Man and nature, which has remained until today a source of inspiration for architects and designers in doing their jobs.

The Xianling Tomb is on the suburbs of Zhongxiang City, Hubei Province, central China. The parents of Emperor Jiajing of the Ming Dynasty were buried together in this tomb, which has green mountains behind it and a river flowing past its front — a place with perfect geomantic omens, indeed. Structures in the mausoleum are arranged in neat order at different heights on the slope of a hill, which at the same time are in perfect harmony with the mountains and rivers in the area. The size and decorations of this tomb are the same as those of any imperial mausoleum of the dynasty, even though its male occupier had never been an emperor himself.

In 1521, Emperor Wuzong, the tenth of the Ming Dynasty, died without a son. One of his nephews was chosen to succeed him and was enthroned as Emperor Jiajing. The new emperor's dead father was a prince and, therefore, was not entitled to a tomb as large and luxurious as an emperor's tomb. Despite opposition from his court officials, Emperor Jiajing honored his father as a dead emperor and had his tomb renovated in accordance with the standards for the tomb of an emperor. While resembling an imperial tomb in size, decoration and layout, Xianling is unique of its own. Instead of being straight, the Divine Road in front of the tomb is winding like the Chinese dragon. The walls surrounding the tomb area form a design in the shape of a gourd-like bottle.

The Qing Dynasty (1644-1911) was China's last feudal dynasty. It had two imperial burial sites, about 100 kilometers to east and west of the capital, Beijing, separately.

Emperors of the Qing Dynasty could not be more painstaking in selecting, when still alive, the sites where they were to be buried after they died. Geological, hydrological, climate and all other natural conditions at the potential burial sites were carefully investigated. No effort was spared to

302

ensure that the tomb structures to be built would be in perfect harmony with the surrounding mountains and rivers. Under the standing rules of the Qing Dynasty, if a queen died before the emperor, she was to be buried together with her husband in the same imperial tomb. If she outlived the emperor, she would have a tomb of her own built near the emperor's tomb, provided her tomb must be smaller in size.

The east imperial burial ground in Zunhua County, Hebei Province, north China, has tombs for five emperors, along with tombs for four queens, five imperial concubines and one princess. The 15 tombs are arranged in strict accordance with the hierarchical system. The tomb of an emperor is placed in the center, with the tomb of his queen close by and tombs of his concubines farther away.

Emperor Shunzhi (1638-1661) was the second emperor of the Qing Dynasty and the first to rule China after the Ming Dynasty was overturned in 1644. His tomb, Xiaoling, sits astride the axis line of the east imperial burial site, with tombs of the four other emperors fanning out in order of their seniority in the imperial family. This was meant to suggest that the junior emperors were performing their filial duties to their fathers or grandfathers. The divine roads in front of the queens' tombs are always connected with the divine roads in front of their husbands' tombs. Moreover, the divine roads of the four emperors after Emperor Shunzhi are all connected with the divine road of Emperor Shunzhi's tomb. The road system was intended to show that the imperial family would last forever.

Here is a brief account of the tombs of four other Qing emperors at the east imperial burial site:

The Jingling Mausoleum is occupied by Emperor Kangxi (1654-1722), son of Emperor Shunzhi, who ran supreme over China for 61 years, longer than any other emperor of the dynasty. Emperor Kangxi had to his credit the last period of national prosperity in China's feudal society.

The Yuling Mausoleum is where Emperor Qianlong (1711-1799) is buried. Emperor Qianlong, who was Emperor Kangxi's grandson, ruled China for 60 years before he abdicated in favor of his son, and then held the title of honor "super-emperor' for three years, until he died at 89. The national prosperity continued under his reign. A devoted believer of Buddhism, he had many relieves on Buddhist themes carved in his underground palace.

The Dingling Mausoleum belongs to Emperor Xianfeng (1831-1861), who was on the throne for just 11 years. China was facing domestic trouble and foreign invasion during his reign. A lot of old material had to be used to construct his tomb due to depletion of the national treasury, and his tomb was not as good in quality as those of the emperors before him.

The Huiling Mausoleum is where Emperor Tongzhi (1856-1874) was buried. Emperor Tongzhi was the only son of Empress Dowager Cixi (1835-1908). He died at 19, and was the shortest-lived emperor of the Qing Dynasty. China was in financial difficulties at the time and his tomb was constructed in great haste. As a result, the wood structure of the ground palace decayed in just 21 years, which had to be torn apart and reconstructed.

The Zhaoxiling Mausoleum belongs to Empress Dowager Xiaozhuang, mother of Emperor Shunzhi and grandmother of Emperor Kangxi. She assisted the two successive emperors in governing the country when they were young. Historians agree that the empress dowager was an outstanding stateswoman in the early Qing Dynasty.

Empress Dowager Cixi, the de facto ruler of China for 48 years, is also buried at the east imperial burial site. Her mausoleum is called Dingdong. Empress Dowager Cixi was originally an imperial concubine of Emperor Xianfeng. After the emperor died, she seized the country's supreme power through a coup. She was not satisfied with the ground palace of her tomb built when she was still alive and ordered rebuilding of it. The best materials were used in the reconstruction, which was done in such a refined manner that the palace on the ground is the most luxurious and magnificent imperial burial structure for the Ming and Qing dynasties.

Burial rules require that a son should be buried side by side with his father. However, Emperor Yongzheng, who succeeded Emperor Kangxi, held that the east imperial site was not good enough in terms of "*feng shui*", and he chose a site for himself, which was to become the west imperial burial site in Yixian County, Hebei Province. His son, Emperor Qianlong, should have had his tomb built at the same site. Emperor Qianlong, however, believed that if emperors after him all had themselves buried at the west imperial site, the east site would eventually be deserted. So he made up his mind to have himself buried at the east site after he died. Furthermore, he established a rule for emperors after him to follow, to the effect that if father was buried at the east site, the son must be buried at the west site.

Tombs at the west site are almost the same as those at the east site in layout. There are altogether 14 tombs at the west site, including the tombs for four emperors.

The Tailing Maosoleum, which belongs to Emperor Yongzheng, was built in 1730. As the first tomb at the west imperial burial site, its layout, size and shape met all the geomantic requirements. It is the largest imperial tomb at the west imperial burial site.

The Changling Mausoleum is occupied by Emperor Jiaqing, son of Emperor Qianlong. It is similar to the Tailing Mausoleum in size.

Emperor Daoguang is the occupier of the Muling Mausoleum, which was built in 1831. The country was in financial difficulties at the time. To advocate thrift, Emperor Daoguang cancelled the building of some structures in his mausoleum.

The Chongling Mausoleum is occupied by Emperor Guangxu. It was built in 1909 and turned out to be the last imperial tomb built in China.

302 Photo shows an ornamental column erected in front of an imperial mausoleum. The tower behind the column shelters a stone tablet dedicated to the dead emperor.

303 An aerial view of the East Imperial Tombs of the Qing Dynasty (1644-1911). Five emperors, four queens, five imperial concubines and one princess are buried at the site.

303

304

305

306

307

304 The Mausoleum of Emperor Shunzhi (1638-1661). It sits astride the axis line that cuts through the Qing Dynasty's east imperial burial ground in the middle. Shunzhi is the second emperor of the dynasty and the first to rule from Beijing after the Manchurian army unified China.

305 The mausoleum belongs to the parents of Emperor Jiajing of the Ming Dynasty. The male occupier of the tomb was not an emperor. Despite that, he was buried the way an emperor was because his son had succeeded the throne.

306 This is just a small part of an imperial mausoleum, but its extravagance suffices to explain why it took years or even decades to build an imperial mausoleum.

307 The dragon was the logo of the emperor and the phoenix, of the queen. So the dragon paired with the phoenix is the theme of most stone carvings found in imperial mausoleums.

308 The Divine Avenue that leads to the tomb of Emperor Shunzhi.

308

309

310

311

309 The mausoleum of Empress Dowager Cixi (1835-1908). The empress dowager was the de facto ruler of China for 48 years, and her tomb is the most luxurious and magnificent of the imperial burial structure for the Ming and Qing dynasties.

310 The main hall of the mausoleum of Emperor Qianlong (1711-1799) of the Qing Dynasty.

311 The Mausoleum of Emperor Yongzheng. It is the largest and most imposing imperial burial structure at the west imperial burial site of the Qing Dynasty.

312 Emperor Qianlong was a devoted follower of Buddhism. On his order, the underground palace where he was to stay after death was made an underground niche for Buddha worshipping. Photo shows a stone relief of the Buddhist Goddess of Mercy in his underground palace.

313 Emperor Qianlong's underground palace.

312

313

314

315

314 Here is a glimpse of the mausoleum for Zhu Di, the third emperor of the Ming Dynasty, and his queen surnamed Xu. It is the first and also the largest of the 13 Ming tombs built near Beijing.

315 Photo shows the underground palace shared by Zhu Xujun, the 13th emperor of the Ming Dynasty, and his two queens.

316 Photo shows the "imperial guard of honor" along the Divine Avenue leading to the tomb shared by Zhu Yuanzhang, the founding emperor of the Ming dynasty, his queen surnamed Ma.

317 Photo shows the interior of the main hall of the mausoleum for Emperor Zhu Di, which is 1,956 square meters large. Pay attention to those huge columns, which are in fact whole trunks of the precious nanmu tree.

316

317

Yungang Grottoes

Yungang Grottoes are 16 kilometers west of Datong City in North China' s Shanxi Province, which was the capital of the North Wei Dynasty (385-534), a political regime established by an ethnic minority group. The dynasty ruled areas to the north of the Yellow River, during the Period of North and South Dynasties when China was divided.

Work began in 460 on caves for worshipping of Buddhism, on order of Emperor Wencheng. Himself a devoted believer of the religion, his majesty accepted a proposal on the project from an eminent monk named Tan Yao. It was already more than 400 years since Buddhism found its way into China, and Buddha worshipping had by then become popular throughout the country.

More than 40,000 workers and artists, including Buddhists from the Kingdom of Lions, or what is now Sri Lanka, took part in the building until 494 when the Northern Wei Dynasty moved its capital to Luoyang, central China. By then, the slope of the Yungang Hill had been turned into a beehive of grottoes about one kilometer long. Of these, 53 have been preserved to this day, in which 1,200 niches and 51,000 Buddhist statues are counted.

Terrain divides the grottoes on the hill into three natural but neat clusters, the east, central and west. Caves in the east area mostly house pagodas, and are thus called "pagoda caves". Most of the caves in the central area have front and rear chambers, with the main Buddha figures sitting in the middle and relieves carved on the ceilings and walls. Caves in the west area are smaller, and in some of these niches are placed.

The five grottoes built under monk Tan Yao' s supervision are in the central area. These grottoes, now serial numbered 16-20, were built in the first phase of the project, which took five years to complete. Each grotto houses an imposing, awe-inspiring Buddha statue, the tallest being 16.8 meters high and the shortest, 13.5 meters. The five Buddha statues were in fact modeled on the images of the dynasty's first five emperors. What merits special mention is the Buddha statue in Grotto No. 20, which is the image of Emperor Wencheng, Monk Tan Yao's most staunch supporter. The cave that once housed the statue is gone due to wind and rain erosion over so many centuries. The statue, now in the open, bears a merciful, serene facial expression, for which it is dubbed as the "goodwill ambassador" of Yungang. Although the looks of the statues in the five caves bear resemblance to the emperors, their dress style, hair buns and decorations on their clothes betray influence of foreign cultures. These statues, to be more precise, look much the same as those found in Central Asia and India.

Grotto building continued after monk Tan Yao died, on an even larger scale as the dynasty was enjoying an economic boom. Grottoes built during this period are the most magnificent at Yungang, mostly with square floors and front

318

and rear chambers. In some caves there are square pagodas, and the carvings there are much more diverse in theme than those in caves dug previously. Moreover, statues there look more Chinese and secular, a fact described by researchers as representing a watershed in the development of China's grotto art.

Almost all the grottoes in the east area were built in pairs, due to what historians call "political reasons". Emperor Xiaowen, who was crowned in the year 471, was known for his success in restructuring the dynasty's political system by taking the political system practiced by the Han Chinese as model. His reform was so thorough that even the life style of the Han ethnic was followed. Nevertheless, in the first 20 years of his reign, it was his grandmother, Empress Dowager Feng, who called the tune behind the curtain. As the grotto building was ordered and largely financed by the emperor, it was natural for the imperial family to have double caves dug, one for blessing of the emperor and the other, for blessing of the empress dowager.

Of the caves dug during this period, one stands out as the largest in size but with the fewest statues. The cave, on a slope 25 meters high and 50 meters wide, has a statue only two centimeters tall, smaller than any other statue found at Yungang. Also found in the cave are engraved inscriptions with 366 Chinese characters. Produced on August 30, 483, the inscriptions tell the story of how a group of 54 Buddhist believers set up a collective fund for building of Buddhist statues. These were the oldest record about the building of Yungang Grottoes, and also the most elaborate in terms of the number of characters. Moreover, the characters are rated as top-rate calligraphic works.

Caves No. 5 and No. 6, however, are the most splendid and most typical of the grottoes at Yungang. A four-story wooden tower built 340 years ago stands in front of the caves. With the rails painted red and green tiles, the tower has five chambers on four stories. Standing on the top story of the tower, one would have the feeling of being in the land of Buddha. The largest Buddha statue at Yungang, 17 meters tall, is housed in Cave No. 5. The statue has a large enough lap for 120 people to stand on it, and the feet can each "accommodate" 12 people. Cave No. 6 has the greatest artistic value. It is in fact a treasure house of Buddhist artworks - sculptures, statues and murals of Buddhist gods and goddess, auspicious birds and animals, beautiful flowers and exotic plants, as well as images of those who sponsored the building of the grotto. They are everywhere, from the floor up to the ceiling.

Two major types of artistic images are found in caves that form the east area of Yungang. Images of the two most important guardian gods of Buddhism, Vishnu and Siva, belong to the first type. The former, with five heads and six arms, is depicted as riding on a peacock and the latter, with three heads and eight arms, as riding on a bull. The peacock symbolizes wisdom, and the bull, good harvests. In artistic style, the statues are rated as unique, in that they bear explicit evidence to influence of both Chinese and foreign cultures.

Flying goddesses fall into the second type. These are found in Caves No. 9 and 10. Dancing gracefully while flying in the sky, the goddesses are as beautiful as those found in the Dunhuang Grottoes.

Cave No. 12 features carvings of musicians and dancers who are performing to celebrate attainment of Buddhahood by Sakyamuni, founder of Buddhism. The "artists", so to speak, are in costumes of ethnic minority groups in north China, and their musical instruments are mostly foreign. Together, they create a scene that cannot be more spectacular.

Caves dug after Emperor of Xiaowen moved his dynasty's capital to Luoyang were no longer imperial shrines for Buddha worshipping. Caves built with donations from aristocrats and Buddhist monks in the old capital are smaller than those built in the past. Most statues in such caves are largely Chinese in artistic style, which are seen by researchers as the prelude to the kind of artistic creation that characterizes Longmen Grottoes.

Yungang Grottoes have the largest collection of grotto artworks in China. The site was inscribed on the UNESCO list of World Natural Heritage in 2001.

319

318 Digging began in 460 on caves No. 16-20 with support from emperor of the North Wei Dynasty. Here is head of a Buddha statue in Cave No. 16.

319 This Buddha statue in Cave No. 20 is 13 meters high. It is valued for being representative of the Yungang grotto art.

320

320 Flying angels scattering flowers from the sky. The relief is found on the ceiling of Cave No. 10. When Buddha gives a lecture, so goes the story, angels will dance in the sky and scatter flowers.

321

322

321 Mahevara, a Buddhist guardian god, in Cave 8. It is depicted as having three heads and eight arms and riding on a white bull.

322 Bohisattvas and some disciples in Cave No. 18. These relieves are masterpieces created in the early phase for building of Yungang Grottoes.

323

324

323 Carvings in Cave No. 12 depict art performances in celebration of Sakyamuni's attainment of Buddhahood. The cave is therefore known as the "cave of music".

324 Caves from No. 9 to No. 13 were dug at the end of the 5th century, and the carvings were painted in 1891. Photo shows Cave No. 9, which is partitioned into two chambers. The smallest Buddha at Yungang, two centimeters tall, is found here.

325

326

325 The cross-legged statue of Maitreya in Cave 13 is 13 meters high. It has a strongman carved under his arm, which serves to support the statue while producing a decorative effect.

326 A series of 33 "pictures" in Cave No. 6 tells the story of Sakyamuni from his birth to his attainment of Buddhahood.

327 Seven Buddha statues are enshrined in Cave No. 11. They are "dressed" the same way as aristocrats in south China at the time, indicating that China's grotto art had already become increasingly Chinese and secular when these statutes were produced.

327 ▶

Sanjiang, Where Three Mighty Rivers Run Abreast

Back in 1985, a UNESCO official was stunned when, examining a satellite remote sensing map, he found three most mighty rivers run abreast somewhere in southwest China, at 98° - 100°30' E. and 25°30' - 29° N. Knowledgeable and highly experienced, the official instantly realized that the area is most likely a natural wonder with a great scientific value.

Shortly after it was notified of the finding, the Chinese government sent experts to the area for field study. In 1998, the Sanjiang (three-river) area, 34,000 square kilometers all told, where the Nujiang, Lancang and Jinsha rivers are aligned from west to east, was designated a scenic site under state-level protection. Then, on July 2, 2003, its core area, 17,000 square kilometers large, came to be inscribed on the UNESCO List of World Natural Heritage.

The Sanjiang area encompasses parts of the Lijiang Prefecture, Diqing Tibet Autonomous Prefecture and Nujiang Lili Autonomous Prefecture in Yunnan Province. The three rivers, Nujiang, Lancang and Jinsha, all originate from the Tanggula Mountains on the Qinghai-Tibet Plateau, the "roof of the world", cutting through towering mountain ranges as they run southward roughly in parallel for about 170 kilometers. The crow-fly distance is only 18.6 kilometers between the closest sections of the Nujiang and Lancang rivers, and the shortest slant line measures no more than 66. 3 kilometers from the Lancang to the Jinsha.

Overlooking the Sanjiang area from aboard an airplane, we can't help marveling a scenic wonder attributed by scientists to the Himalaya mountain-building movement that took place some 60 million years ago. Greeting our eyes are those snaking mountain ranges, those snow-clad rolling peaks, those lush green forests, those marshlands dazzling with color, as well as those plateau lakes shining bright under the sun. Sandwiched in between four mountain ranges, the rivers cut through valleys 2,000 to 4,000 meters deep. Likewise, the Gaoligong, Nushan (also known as Biluo), Yunling and Greater-Lesser mountain ranges snake in parallel from west to east.

As it flows eastward, the Jinsha River, into which the Yalong, Dadu and Jialing rivers empty, expands into the upper section of the Yangtze, the longest river in China and the fourth longest in the world. It makes an abrupt round about turn at Shigu Township in Lijiang Prefecture and then runs all the way to east coast of the Pacific. Sandwiched in between the Yulong and Haba snow mountains is the Tiger Jumping Canyon, roaring as the river washes down, which can be heard several kilometers away. The canyon is 16 kilometers long, with the narrowest section only 30 meters wide while the valley is as deep as 3,000 meters.

The Nujiang River virtually falls down in between the Gaoligong and Biluo mountains, on an elevation so steep that dangerous rapids are found everywhere along its course. Cliffs flanking the river are precipitous - almost standing erect, to be exact - so precipitous that, as the local saying goes, "even wild goats and monkeys find it impossible to climb." This river is an international waterway, the upper section of the Thanlwinn River of Myanmar that empties into the Indian Ocean.

The Lancang, the fifth longest river in China, is the upper section of the Mekong River that snakes through Myanmar, Laos, Thailand, Kampuchea and Vietnam before it empties into the South China Sea. The section of the river in between the snow-clad Yunling and Biluo mountains features a relatively flat terrain even though the valley ranges

328

from 2,000 to 3,000 meters in depth, where beautiful villages are seen here and there.

Towering snow mountains, thriving forests, magnificent valleys and canyons up to 4,000 meters deep - these are just some of the most salient features of the Sanjiang area with four mountain ranges standing side by side and three mighty rivers running abreast. Scientists believe that the area resulted from a collision of the India Plate with the Euro-Asian Plate some 4,000 years ago, an aftermath of the Himalaya mountain building movement that took place 20 million years earlier. The force generated by the tectonic drama is beyond our wildest imagination, evidenced by those typical deep sea rocks found atop mountains that rise 4,000 meters above sea level. The Sanjiang area boasts the greatest geological diversity in the world, featuring everything in the North Hemisphere except deserts and seas.

Altogether, the area has 118 peaks perennially covered with snow, which rise 5,000 meters above sea level or even higher. Of these, Mt. Meili merits special mention. Local Tibetans regard it as sacred, to which access by mortals is forbidden. A glacier, more than 4,000 meters long, snakes all the way down, meeting forests at 2,650 meters above sea level. It is in fact on the lowest elevation among all glaciers in the North Hemisphere. The peak of Mt. Meili, known as Mt. Kawagebo, stands 6,740 meters above sea level and is the highest in the Sanjiang area. Though 2,100 meters lower than Mt. Qomolangma, the "peak of the earth", Mt. Kawagebo has remained virgin, forbidden to mountaineering as it is covered with snow and shrouded in heavy fogs and clouds all the year round and downpours and windstorms frequently occur. In January 1991, a team of 17 Chinese and Japanese climbers died while trying to conquer it.

Here in the Sanjiang area there is one more geological wonder known as the "red stone landform" - purplish red cliffs resulting from erosion of sandy rock strata over millions of years. Such cliffs are scenic wonders under the blue sky, with snow-clad mountains and deep forests in the background. The red stone landform in Liming is rated as the largest and best developed in the world, and also on the highest elevation. Liming nestles deep in Mt. Laojun 140 kilometers from Lijiang. By the way, the old town of Lijiang City is a site on the UNECO List of World Cultural Heritage.

A bio-diversity stems from a meteorological diversity, both characterizing the Sanjiang area. All the way up from the Nujiang Valley to Mt. Kawaboge, the peak of the area, on an elevation of no more than 6,000 meters one travels in succession through the South subtropical, Central subtropical, North subtropical, mild temperate, temperate, cold temperate and frigid zones. Nature endows the area with a greatest bio-diversity in the world. The area accounts for only 0.4 percent of China's land mass, but thriving there are more than 6,000 higher plant species, 20 percent of the total identified so far in the country. The area also has one fourth of the animal species in China. Included are species left over from the Quaternary Period from one million years ago, which are known for their scientific value. Moreover, it is a most important habitat of the Yunnan golden-hair monkey, a "national treasure" as rare and precious as the giant panda. The Sanjiang area turns out a "sea of flowers" in spring, where more than 200 azalea varieties are identified. For all this, the Chinese Academy of Sciences has designated it to top a list of 17 key areas for protection of bio-diversity. Moreover, the area has come to be known as the "greatest pool of biological genes" for the world.

Far back in 1883, French missionaries arrived in the area to collect plant and animal specimens. Basing himself on their findings, Professor Balfour at the Royal Botanical Conservatory in Edinburg of the United Kingdom concluded in 1904 that plants growing on mountains in the northwest of China's Yunnan Province were most promising for growth in British gardens. Then British scientists arrived on request of the professor. In making technical assessment on the area for its entry into the UNESCO List of World Natural Heritage, experts with the International Union for Conservation of Nature said that it is difficult to find another area good enough to match Sanjiang in terms of ecological and landform diversity.

The Sanjiang area is home to 14 of the 56 ethnic groups in China, with an aboriginal population of 800,000, who speak different languages, have different religious beliefs and follow different folkways. Their ethnic identities, however, are largely preserved. Even though cut off from the rest of the world by the treacherous terrain, it was already magnetic to scientists, adventurers and travelers a long, long time ago. Joseph Locke, an American traveler who wrote for the *National Geographic*, lived in northwest Yunnan for more than 20 years in the early 20th century.

In 1933, the word "Shangri-La" appeared in the British novel the *Disappearing Horizon*. It is a dreamland owned by both humans and deities, where people live in perfect harmony with nature. Textual research and field studies have led to the conclusion that author James Hilton's inspiration came from areas in Yunnan inhabited by ethnic Tibetans, including what is now Diqing Tibet Autonomous Prefecture.

328 Photo shows the Mingyong Glacier, about 4,000 meters long, which features the lowest elevation among glaciers found all over the North Hemisphere.

329 Photo shows the "first bend of the Yangtze". As it flows from north to south, the Jinsha River takes a round about turn at Shigu Town in the Lijiang area.

329

330 Here we see Mt. Miancimu, the peak of the Meili Mountains, and ethnic Tibetan villages at its foot. "Miancimu" means "daughter of the God of Seas", and for that, Mt. Miancimu is also known as the "mountain of the beauty".

331 A glimpse of the Baimang Xueshan Nature Preserve in the Sanjiang Area, which is reputed for a wealth of geological ruins and diverse landforms.

332 Photo shows the "first bend of Nujiang River" at Bingzhongluo Township, Gongshan Dulong Autonomous County.

333 Snow-clad mountains in the Sanjiang area.

332

333

334

335

334 An overhead cable in Nujang Canyon

335 Lancangjiang Canyon

336 A glimpse of Mt. Kawagebo, the "forbidden" peak of the Meili mountains.

337 A typical scene at Liming with the red stone landform.

336

337

338

339

338 The Songzanlin Monastery in Diqing, the largest shrine for the Tibetan School of Buddhism in Yunnan province. It was built in 1679.

339 Lake Napa, meaning "lake at the side of a forest" in the Tibetan language. Most parts of this plateau lake turn into grassy marshlands or marshes in the dry season.

340 Fir trees and azalea flowers in shrubs. The photo was taken at the Mt. Qianhu Nature Preserve.

341 Fairy primroses.

342 Flowers of meconopsis. Altogether, 49 varieties of the meconopsis family have been identified across the world. China has more than any other country, which grow mostly in places 3,000 meters above sea level or higher in northwest Yunnan Province.

343 Plateau grassy marshland.

344 Yunnan golden-hair monkeys.

340

341

342

343

344

图片摄影

于　宁：085 092 109
于云天：082
车文龙：218 220 221
邓根宝：076 081
王刁年：097
王文波：003 064 068
王庆伦：259 267
王达军：083 089 090 107 112 113 175 269
王保平：037 038 039 040 041 043 047 048 049 050
王建军：008 209
王　敏：270 271 274 277
王德全：027 028 035
王德英：316
包承立：275
台　威：025
田捷砚：141 170 171 179
叶用才：001 314
华仲明：002 010
江明义：272
刘力群：071 304
刘文敏：138
刘　臣：125
刘启俊：072 315 317
刘宪忱：011
刘建华：212
齐凤臣：007 187 238 295 319
孙永学：026 034 181
孙伟忠：194
孙志江：053
孙树明：172 174 260 261 302 303 306 310
朱恩光：330 331 332 334 335 338 339 340
陈　宇：013 114
陈克寅：115 121
陈宝森：116 117 119 120 122 123
陈　锦：177 273
杜泽泉：018 145
谷维恒：087 094
何世尧：088
李少白：017 021 294 308 309
李　元：176
李　江：222 305
邰永东：105
汪传树、陈守清：151 152 154 155 157
严钟义：096 098 233 284 289 290 291 318 320 321 322 326
杨学飞：336
杨学光：333
杨秀云：210
杨绍全：108
杨　茵：148 160
张仁东：033
张云磊：029
张永富：075 078 079
张国田：182 186
张振光：195 207
张海雁：280 288
张海雁、员新华：323 324 327
张肇基：014 016 022 065 066 067 226 231 232 235 236 239
周仁德：196 200 201 202 203 206
周　利：329
周沁军：006 080 133 134 135 268 281 283 285 286
罗文发：020 263 307 312 313
罗克恒：158 159 161 165 166 168 169
罗哲文：012
庞守义：030 127 128 129 132
林晶华：137
宫　正：163
侯贺良：031 126 130
侯晋封：069 070（供图）
胡国钦：245 251 252 255 256
姜　平：178 264 278
姜景余：213
茹遂初：051 052 054 055 056 057 058 059 060 061 062 063 095 099 104 183 185 188 189 190 191 192 211 216 217 230 237 265
姚天新：223 225 227 229 240 242
赵　勇：243 249 253 254
奚志农：328 337 341 342 343 344
郭　宜：266
高屯子：086 106 110
高明义：024 241 287
高榴松：193 204
夏居宪、郭燕：036 042 044 045 046
袁学军：084 184 228 257 262
袁廉民：073 077 296
鄂　毅：173 208 246 325
黄加法：244
黄　海：248 250
黄韬朋：005 015 032 136 279 311
鲁昌麟：258
银道禄：147 149 150 153 156
谢新发：100 101 102 103 111 139 142 143 144 146 167 180 197 198 199 205 219 247 276 282 298
蒙　紫：019 023 074 118 124 140 224 234
谭　明：091 093 131
熊元生：162 164
翟东风：004 009
樊炎冰：214 215 292 293 297 299 300 301